P9-DHF-292

Shelbyville-Shelby County
Public Library

437367

Madeleine L'Engle

Banned, Challenged, and Censored

Marilyn McClellan

Enslow Publishers, Inc.
40 Industrial Road
Box 398
Berkeley Heights, NJ 07922
USA

http://www.enslow.com

*This book is dedicated to Madeleine L'Engle
in appreciation for the countless lives she has touched
throughout her long and amazing career.*

Copyright © 2008 by Marilyn McClellan

All rights reserved.

No part of this book may be reproduced by any means without the written permission of the publisher.

Library of Congress Cataloging-in-Publication Data

McClellan, Marilyn.
  Madeleine L'Engle : banned, challenged, and censored / Marilyn McClellan.
     p. cm.—(Authors of banned books)
  Includes bibliographical references (p.   ) and index.
  ISBN-13: 978-0-7660-2708-4
  ISBN-10: 0-7660-2708-2
  1. L'Engle, Madeleine—Criticism and interpretation—Juvenile literature. 2. Challenged books—Juvenile
literature. 3. Prohibited books—Juvenile literature. 4. Censorship—Juvenile literature. I. Title.
  PS3523.E55Z74 2008
  813'.54—dc22

                         2007015134

Printed in the United States of America

10 9 8 7 6 5 4 3 2 1

To Our Readers: We have done our best to make sure that all Internet addresses in this book were active and appropriate when we went to press. However, the author and publisher have no control over and assume no liability for the material available on those Internet sites or on other Web sites they may link to. Any comments or suggestions can be sent by e-mail to comments@enslow.com or to the address on the back cover.

Illustration Credits: Courtesy of Crosswicks, Ltd., pp. 1, 10, 57, 60, 64, 75, 99, 126, back cover; Holtzbrinck Publishers, p. 86; Donel McClellan, p. 4; Office for Intellectual Freedom, American Library Association, p. 113; Photos.com, pp. 25, 39; Courtesy of Luci Shaw, p. 131.

Cover Illustration: Courtesy of Crosswicks, Ltd.

Contents

Chapter 1

Meet Madeleine L'Engle

(Author's note: Madeleine L'Engle died on September 6, 2007, as this book was going to press.)

Although it is not beyond belief that beloved authors sometimes have harsh critics, not too many have books written expressly to discredit them in the eyes of their readers. This puts American literature favorite Madeleine L'Engle in a special class. She has been damned in print for being manipulative and intimidating. In a letter to his fellow members, one church official wrote that L'Engle's writings are "repulsive, dangerous, subversive and treacherous."[1] She has been said to deliver a message that is "highly dangerous and seductive ... to the young and old alike."[2] She has been accused of adding her own flavor to the Christian gospel that is delicately seasoned "with a pinch of rat poison."[3]

L'Engle is a prolific author who has written more than sixty books since beginning her long and successful career in the 1940s. She has won many awards for her writing and is considered one of the foremost children's writers of the twentieth century. Although older fans delight in her many fiction and nonfiction books for teenagers and adults, L'Engle is probably best known for her children's books. Her most popular children's book is the Newbery Medal winner, *A Wrinkle in Time*, which has been translated into fifteen languages and has sold more than 6 million copies. Although this book was published many years ago, in 1962, it continues to have a wide appeal for young people. To their delight, as well as the delight of many of their parents and grandparents who also enjoyed the book when they were young, it was made into a TV special and aired in 2004, more than forty years after it was written.

However, as is the case with all artists and writers, it is true that not everyone understands or appreciates L'Engle's work. According to the Office for Intellectual Freedom of the American Library Association, *A Wrinkle in Time* ranked twenty-second among the most frequently challenged books of the 1990s.[4] There have also been multiple attempts to remove L'Engle's book *Many Waters* from the schoolhouse shelves. As an author of challenged books, L'Engle is in good company with Mark Twain, J. K. Rowling, Katherine Paterson, Judy Blume, and Maurice Sendak. All of these—among many others—are authors whose books are not acceptable to people who believe that children should not be exposed to certain themes or elements in stories. Often the groups behind the censorship attempts share similar concerns or values, although not always. In L'Engle's case, her censors usually disagree with her on religious grounds. And these concerns do not apply only to her literature that is read by children. Some of her strongest critics are concerned about her books that appeal to adults.

The Controversy

Religion is a sensitive topic even for those who do not consider themselves religious. Entire cultures are driven by the primary religion of the area. Although many different religions are observed in the United States, Christianity has been the principal religion in the nation. Children who grow up in

The Most Frequently Challenged Books of 1990–2000

1. Scary Stories (series) by Alvin Schwartz
2. *Daddy's Roommate* by Michael Willhoite
3. *I Know Why the Caged Bird Sings* by Maya Angelou
4. *The Chocolate War* by Robert Cormier
5. *Adventures of Huckleberry Finn* by Mark Twain
6. *Of Mice and Men* by John Steinbeck
7. Harry Potter (series) by J. K. Rowling
8. *Forever* by Judy Blume
9. *Bridge to Terabithia* by Katherine Paterson
10. Alice (series) by Phyllis Reynolds Naylor[5]

America are familiar with Christmas and Easter celebrations even if they do not observe these holidays. Many of the country's social and political structures are based upon Judeo-Christian ethics. In other countries, of course, the cultures are affected by other belief systems. For example, children who live in China would celebrate the Chinese New Year and be familiar with Buddha's birthday and the Qing Ming festival in spring. Many homes would have photos of ancestors and incense burning on altars.

Religious preference is dependent on many different factors. What worshipers believe, the form of worship, the comfort level with the governing structure, the

L'Engle's most popular children's book, A Wrinkle in Time, has been translated into fifteen languages and has sold more than 6 million copies.

socioeconomic level, and the welcome they receive are just a few factors that draw people to organized religion. Within most religions, beliefs are on a continuum that stretches from the very conservative to the very liberal. There is a wide range of beliefs within Christianity. L'Engle and those who disagree with her writings are at opposite ends of the spectrum.

L'Engle has always been aware that some Christian readers are critical of what they believe are her heretical ideas. She knows that people have written books and articles analyzing and denouncing her, that sermons have been preached against her in churches, and that attempts have been made to remove her books from libraries. She has even experienced the frustration of having people heckle her when she has lectured at conferences and classes. But when a friend called her one day to warn her about a radio program whose participants were discussing her work, she was unprepared for the fury her critics unleashed against her. L'Engle writes:

> It was a very strange sensation to listen to a spewing out of hate, a septic vilification of me and everything I believe. My response was instinctively visceral, as though someone were plunging a knife in my intestines and twisting it.[6]

The speaker on the show was accusing L'Engle of spreading a "New Age" philosophy. These ideas, according to the speaker, undermined the basic truths of the Christian faith. What disturbed her most was that L'Engle was a popular writer and had a strong influence on many Christian readers, including children. Among L'Engle's harshest critics are authors Brenda Scott and Samantha Smith. In their book *Trojan Horse: How the New Age Movement Infiltrates the Church*, they write: "Despite her blatant denial of the basic tenets of the faith, Madeleine L'Engle's influence has deeply penetrated mainstream Christianity." Scott and Smith feared that L'Engle had introduced dangerous ideas into the church

Madeleine L'Engle, shown here in a publicity photo from 1987, is considered one of the foremost children's authors of the twentieth century.

under the guise of "Christian literature."[7] These were strong, negative statements about such a popular, award-winning author.

L'Engle does not like labels to be attached to her writing. She does not think of herself as a Christian writer, or a children's writer, or any other specific kind of writer. She admits she is a Christian person who writes and who enjoys a wide appeal among different groups of readers. For most of her readers, her religion is not an issue. They read her books because she is an engaging storyteller. However, she does have fans who see her as primarily a religious writer. These readers find L'Engle's books deeply spiritual and inspirational in the way they weave the Christian faith and beliefs into storytelling.

Madeleine L'Engle is no stranger to the Bible. It is part of her daily reading. Not only do biblical references weave through her fiction, but her characters in her novels also face Judeo-Christian dilemmas such as choosing between good and evil, discerning the nature of God, and seeking human redemption or forgiveness for their actions. Her nonfiction reflects her lifelong quest for spiritual truth as well as growth and understanding. Carole F. Chase writes in her book *Madeleine L'Engle, Suncatcher:*

> For almost fifty years, Madeleine L'Engle has been creating out of her beliefs and her life a variegated body of work through which the Light of God is allowed to filter to the millions

of people who read her books.... [She] is not only a storyteller par excellence, but a teacher about God, humanity, and the cosmos.[8]

L'Engle remarks about the religious controversy surrounding the censorship of *A Wrinkle in Time:* "One thing that fascinates me; when it came out, it was hailed as an Evangelical book, a Christian book. Now it is being deplored as a dreadful book. Not a word of it has changed."[9] After hearing the upsetting radio broadcast, she wondered, "Why are those who criticize my writing people who loudly proclaim themselves followers of Christ? Why do others, to my humble awe, find that [my] books lead them to Christ?"[10]

Some fans see L'Engle as a marvelous storyteller, some see her as an inspired and gifted Christian writer, while others find her religious ideas dangerous and wish to prevent people from reading her books. This is a curious dilemma, but not an unusual one for authors. Artists in society are often misunderstood and sometimes inspire controversy, whether they mean to or not. The divisiveness that exists between religious people is certainly not new or even specific to Christianity. For centuries, wars have been fought on all continents both between separate religious groups and within specific religions. Adherents do not always agree on the basic doctrines of their faith or how to celebrate their rites and customs. Sometimes they differ on the interpretation of religious texts. Unfortunately, great conflicts often exist between people of faith.

Differences in religious belief, mixed with other factors such as political unrest or government control, often lie at the heart of the concerns that breed censorship. Throughout history, groups have sought to stem the tide of cultural change. Religious factions wage attacks on those who embrace other faiths. Censors attempt to halt the circulation of new or different ideas. They suppress anything objectionable or offensive to their beliefs as they seek to protect society from what they think are dangerous opinions. Most religious and political censors are fighting for what they hold dear and believe to be true. They believe that certain ideas are not only dangerous, but also can be destructive, and therefore must be controlled.

Christian Fundamentalism

It is impossible to understand Madeleine L'Engle's critics without a basic knowledge of a division that exists within the Christian religion. L'Engle's main critics are Christian fundamentalists. This is a group that believes strongly in a return to what they consider the fundamentals, or basic tenets, of the Christian faith. Christian fundamentalism grew widespread in the beginning of the twentieth century as a reaction to a variety of social changes in America. One of the things that happened during those years was that German biblical scholars were influential in raising questions about the origin of the biblical texts. Using the scientific method, they studied the languages and history that produced the various interpretations of the Bible. By learning more about the cultures that produced the books and the various translations, modern scholars felt that they could more fully understand the Bible. This was a contrast to those Christians who believed that the words in the Bible were not open to interpretation because they were inspired by God.

Also during this period, Charles Darwin's ideas about biological evolution were becoming widely accepted in society. This challenged the literal biblical understanding of the creation of the world. These new ways of thinking about the past were of great concern for some Christian people who believed that the historical truths of the Bible were being challenged. At the same time, the Industrial Revolution had further widened a division between the rich and poor. This caused many Christian churches to call for a broader definition of what it meant to be a Christian. Moving away from the traditional emphasis on a personal faith, they called for religious people to work for justice in the world and the reform of social institutions. Pastors preached sermons that urged members to stretch their faith to look outward, believing that to be a Christian meant to follow Christ's teachings into the world with obligations to help the poor and powerless. Not everyone agreed with this. In response to these trends, one group began to circulate a series of pamphlets reminding Christians of the fundamental tenets of their faith. What emerged from this process was a branch of Christianity that attempts a return to the fundamentals of faith that they believe many Christians abandoned when they embraced the intellectual and cultural changes of the times.

Christian fundamentalism is strong today. It has not developed into a distinct sect within the Christian faith, like Methodists or Catholics, but instead has grown into many different groups within the global society, including some churches, universities, and organizations that strive to bring the "true" religion back into churches, social life, and public policy. Through the years, American fundamentalist organizations have been active in establishing a power base in order to reform important institutions like education. They have elected members to school boards, worked to change textbooks, and challenged the teaching of evolution in the public schools. They strive to keep literature they believe is an insult to their religious principles off of library shelves.

L'Engle is one of the authors that some fundamentalists wish to ban from school classrooms. She is often accused by her critics of being "New Age" because she incorporates telepathy, magic, and nonwestern philosophies into her writings. She writes, "Why am I being accused of being a New Ager? It's beyond me unless meditation, imagination, poetry, joy in the Creator and creation are considered to be New Age."[11] People also criticize her for including ancient religious practices, native rites, and characters who question their faith within her fiction for children.

Some Christian fundamentalists object to L'Engle's use of science. She is an avid reader of scientific literature with an interest in astrophysics, particle physics, and cellular biology. This interest led her to take her characters in *A Wrinkle in Time* "traveling" through space and time, which brought her writing into the world of science fiction and fantasy. L'Engle does not understand why science and religion have to be separate. Differing from the Christian fundamentalists who embrace the literal biblical account of creation, she has no trouble with evolution. She argues that we cannot pin the number of days it took to create the universe into our conception of a day—we cannot fathom God's timeline for the event. How long was a day to God? Pitting science against religion "has never made sense to me. People get their own definitions of God."[12] Another time she wrote, "When we discovered that the earth is not the center of the universe, it didn't change God. It just changed us, and what we think. We have to be willing to allow what we think to change."[13]

Madeleine L'Engle would argue with those who would question the integrity of her faith. She has written that Christianity is in her genes and probably coded in her DNA. She has been immersed in the Bible since her parents read it to her as a child. She was raised as an Episcopalian and continues to belong to that Protestant denomination, which, according to her, is a branch of Christianity that gives her elbow room to ask questions while providing a long and literary structure to her faith.[14] But, curiously, throughout her writing career, she has been welcomed as a lecturer and teacher of writing by a wide variety of both conservative and

16

liberal Christian denominations. A book by Claris Van Kuiken—*Battle to Destroy Truth*—was written about her disagreement with the pastors of her evangelical church because they refused to agree that L'Engle's writings denied the essential Christian teachings.[15] This provides a glimpse into the divisions of thought that exist even within Christian fundamentalism.

L'Engle regularly addresses her critics in her many nonfiction books and in public talks. In a lecture to the Library of Congress on November 16, 1983, she said, "We need to dare disturb the universe by not being manipulated or frightened by ... groups who assume the right to insist that if we do not agree with them, not only do we not understand, but we are wrong."[16] Madeleine L'Engle's philosophy about her critics is written, most succinctly, in an Edwin Markham poem entitled "Outwitted," which she learned by memory in high school:

> *He drew a circle that shut me out—*
> *Heretic, rebel, a thing to flout.*
> *But Love and I had the wit to win:*
> *We drew a circle that took him in.*

Censorship and Society

Every society has customs or laws that regulate cultural activities such as the way people speak or dress, their religious observance, and their artistic expressions. Long before the printing press was introduced, censorship flourished as a method to extinguish ideas that might be dangerous or unacceptable to the establishment. It was not difficult for those in power to decide what people could read, because few people were educated or could read at all. Authorities decided what information and ideas people would have access to. Reproducing manuscripts by hand was difficult and tedious. Mobility from town to town was limited compared to the modern world. Most societies had a long oral tradition that was passed down through the ages. Ideas traveled slowly, and when they did travel, it was usually by the spoken word. The history of censorship wends its way through many cultures, traditions, and political and religious structures.

The Beginning of Censorship

The Greek philosopher Plato and his teacher Socrates are familiar to most students. Socrates is considered one of the first supporters of intellectual freedom as he taught his students to question and reason. Athenian officials decided he was too free a thinker and sentenced him to death for discussing his unorthodox religious ideas with his students. They were afraid he would corrupt the young men who studied with him. Interestingly, his most famous student, Plato, wrote a rationale to support intellectual, religious, and artistic censorship. Plato did not believe that art should be allowed to indoctrinate the young or that people should be exposed to evil or wrong ideas about the gods. Although the Greeks and Romans were societies that encouraged openness and debate, they did practice censorship of unpopular religious or political opinions. For instance, the Roman emperor Caligula tried to suppress the *Odyssey* of Homer because the Greek ideals of freedom expressed in the tales were not acceptable to the Roman government.[1] Another Roman emperor, Constantine, burned theological books that did not support the Christianity he had converted to and adopted as the official religion of the state.

Book burning or confiscation by officials was one method of silencing voices of dissension or unpopular ideas in those early years. Pope Paul IV's 1559 *Index Librorum Prohibitorum*—"Index of Forbidden Books"— was binding on all Roman Catholics who, at that time, represented most of the population of continental

19

Europe.[2] The index lasted almost four hundred years in one form or another until the final edition was issued as late as 1948. In 1231, Pope Gregory IX began the Inquisition. Before this time, the Catholic Church had no structured system to deal with those who disagreed with its teachings. Local authorities who supported the "official religion" of the state assigned official inquirers to look into possible illegal activities such as printing and distributing heretical books. The Inquisition in a variety of forms flourished throughout Europe for hundreds of years and was a primary agency for handling religious and political censorship.

The tedious and sometimes inaccurate method of hand-producing books changed dramatically in 1455. That year, a metalworker, Johannes Gutenberg, produced the Gutenberg Bible and introduced the first printing press that used moveable type. Until that time, printed material could not be mass-produced. As printing became more common in all countries, so did literacy, allowing for the wider spread of information. The circulation of manuscripts not only vastly multiplied, but was also difficult to control. Books that were banned or prohibited in one country could simply be printed and distributed in another country. In 1633, the mathematician Galileo was condemned for heresy by the Roman Inquisition and placed under house arrest because he supported the Copernican system that stated that the sun was the center of the universe. His works were smuggled out of Italy and into Holland, where they were printed and sold.

Censorship and Society

Censorship can happen at any time along the process from writing to publishing. A writer can self-censor and refuse to write or publish at the outset. This might be out of fear for his or her own safety or a reprisal by a group or individual. This is called the "chilling effect" because that is the consequence it has on the freedom of speech. A manuscript can be halted because someone in charge is convinced that the writings may contain dangerous ideas. At the University of Paris in 1342, professors were not allowed to hand any lecture over to the booksellers before it had been examined by the chancellors and the professors of theology. This type of prepublication censorship was common under the early Roman Catholic Church, which would not give its blessing to any publication that did not maintain or support the "one true faith."

Most of the world's religious texts have been banned at one time or another. The Bible is one of the most censored books in history. Perhaps that is because it has been translated countless times and is available in so many languages. William Tyndale was the first person to translate and print the Bible in English. It was printed in Germany and smuggled into England because at that time one had to obtain permission to read a new translation before it was officially accepted by the Church. Tyndale's translation was not well received and was publicly burned by the Catholic Church; Tyndale himself was put to death for heresy in 1536. Other religious texts such as the Talmud, a sacred compilation of writings from ancient Jewish scholars, and the

Qur'an, the sacred book of Islam, have been prohibited and burned, often by Christians who did not agree with beliefs that differed from theirs.

Many famous authors who are revered today were at one time banned from publication. William Shakespeare, Hans Christian Andersen, Elizabeth Barrett Browning, Walt Whitman, and Arthur Conan Doyle are just a small sampling of those whose works were once found unacceptable. In nineteenth-century England, the high price of books led to the growth of circulating libraries. For a modest price, readers were able to borrow the most popular novels of the day. However, the first librarians carefully examined books for crude language or unduly explicit or realistic portrayals of life. Most of the nineteenth century has been called the Victorian Period after the British Queen Victoria, who reigned for almost sixty-four years. The period is known for its strict morality and an emphasis on social mores and proper etiquette. Writers, editors, and publishers were clear about what the public would accept. Often, but fortunately not always, they censored their own publications in order to keep their books in line with the public conscience. However, literary figures such as Mark Twain, Walt Whitman, and Thomas Hardy were published even when considered outrageous by the moral standards of the time.

Political Censorship

Censorship by authority is a strong component of autocratic forms of government, such as dictatorships.

There are numerous historic and contemporary examples where writers who attempted to speak against abuses of power were silenced and their texts were destroyed. Artistic and intellectual freedom remains an issue today in many countries where the free flow of ideas is halted by those in control.

Although political censorship has diminished in Western nations in the last century, some countries have rarely been free of censorship. Russia operated for centuries under the czars, then under one-party

Many famous authors who are revered today—including Shakespeare, Whitman, and Hans Christian Andersen— were at one time banned from publication.

Communist rule until the breakup of the Soviet Union in the late 1980s. It has experienced strict censorship for most of its existence, including events such as the destruction of libraries by the rulers of the Soviet Union in the 1930s. This censorship heightened and extended to all of Russia's occupied countries during the time of Joseph Stalin. All foreign books were banned and the countries were purged of unauthorized publications.[3] Nazi Germany is another example of a country that practiced rigorous political and artistic censorship. Mountains of books offensive to the Nazis were burned by the regime in the 1930s. Not only were works by Jewish authors and others destroyed, but also in occupied countries such as Norway, even "listening to 'foreign' radio or producing, reading or disseminating illegal newspapers was punishable by death," according to Norwegian author Mette Newth.[4] The suppression of artists, writers, and scholars during China's Cultural Revolution in the 1960s is a prime example of a dictatorship deciding who can or cannot have a voice in its society. Millions of citizens died or were imprisoned, and countless ancient works of art such as sculptures, books, and paintings were destroyed.

These are but a few famous examples of countries where a political dictatorship was able to silence all those who speak with a different voice or who appear to be a threat to the ruling power. They are a sad commentary on how a culture can lose its precious historical heritage under tyrannical political regimes. However, as much as they try, dictators have not always been able to stop those who disagree from publishing "underground" works or illegal newspapers in suppressed nations. Manuscripts get smuggled into other countries where they are printed and read. It is almost impossible to smother the freedom of expression.

In the seventeenth century, a poet named Richard Lovelace wrote, "Stone walls do not a prison make, nor iron bars a cage...."[5] Lovelace's words remind us that although a person can be thrown in jail, nothing can imprison ideas. Even today in countries around the world, attacks on the freedom of expression continue. The most famous recent example of this is Salman

Rushdie, a British journalist, who wrote the book *The Satanic Verses*. An Islamic group believed that it was blasphemous, or disrespectful to God. A *fatwa*—a decree by a religious leader—was issued, calling for Rushdie to be assassinated. Human rights organizations around the world report on the continual violent attacks on journalists. More than half the world's

An engraving of a printing office in Antwerp, Belgium, about 1600. The invention of the printing press transformed the way information was spread.

Shelbyville-Shelby County
Public Library

population still lacks a free press or independent newspaper. According to the Committee to Protect Journalists, 134 editors, writers, and photojournalists were imprisoned around the world in 2006.[6] During the same year, the organization reported that fifty-five journalists were killed worldwide in direct connection to their work. Thirty-two of those were attributed to violence in Iraq, and another twenty-seven suspicious deaths are being investigated.[7]

Early Censorship in America

The First Amendment to the United States Constitution reads:

> Congress shall make no law respecting an establishment of religion, or prohibiting the free exercise thereof; or abridging the freedom of speech, or of the press; or the right of the people peaceably to assemble, and to petition the Government for a redress of grievances.

Although the U.S. Constitution does not specifically mention the word "censorship," this amendment protects the freedom of citizens to express their views, even if those views are unpopular. However, the United States has not been free of censorship. Courts have struggled, from the beginning, to interpret the limits to the freedoms granted by the Constitution in view of the best interests of citizens. Challenges arise from political interest groups as well as the government itself, especially during times of national crisis. Organizations

26

such as the American Civil Liberties Union work on behalf of citizens who feel their civil liberties are being threatened.

Over the centuries, most writing suppressed by authorities has been on religious or political grounds. However, in America a great proportion of material has been banned because it was believed to be offensive to society. U.S. customs laws had control over the import of art and literature and could prevent any material that was considered immoral or indecent from entering the country. The United States passed its first obscenity law in 1842 authorizing the Customs Service to confiscate "obscene or immoral" pictures.[8] Lists of banned works existed to help guide state and local law enforcement groups. "Societies for the prevention of vice" sprang up to lobby for stricter state obscenity laws that would protect the public. These were made up of people,

Terms Related to Book Censorship

ban—To remove a book or other material from a library or school curriculum.

bowdlerize—To remove objectionable passages from a written work by shortening, simplifying, or skewing the content.

censor—To prevent the publication or dissemination of material that is considered objectionable, sensitive, or harmful.

challenge—To file a formal protest against the inclusion of a book in a library.

expurgate—To remove objectionable material from a piece of writing.

restict—To limit the circulation of a book to people of a particular age or those who have parental approval.

often philanthropists and social reformers, who felt they were acting as an "enlightened social conscience."[9] The leading enforcer of these laws was Anthony Comstock, who created the New York Society for the Suppression of Vice in 1873. His "Comstock Law" expanded the existing regulations and made it a federal offense to send all indecent publications through the mail. These were described as printed items including illustrations or advertisements that contained "obscene, lewd, or lascivious" material.[10] The U.S. Postal Service was a strong force that kept "dirty" books out of America and controlled the distribution of information on sensitive subjects such as birth control and abortion. Publishers and librarians often cooperated by keeping literature that was offensive to "polite society" off the shelves. This widespread concern about community standards had a dampening effect on writers who wished to market their work. Although James Joyce's famous work *Ulysses* is now considered to be one of the most significant novels of the twentieth century, the U.S. Postal Service seized any copies it could find during the 1920s. Voltaire's *Candide* and Geoffrey Chaucer's *The Canterbury Tales* were two other titles that were banned from entering the country.

Changing Values

The early decades of the twentieth century saw a great deal of cultural change in the United States. The end of the First World War was followed by the breakdown of Prohibition (the period from 1920 to 1933, during which it was illegal to manufacture or sell alcohol). At the same time there was enormous growth in the movie industry, the magazine and newspaper trade, and the popularity of the stage. The cultural climate in America began to change, and opposition to any censorship grew. By the end of the 1920s, movies were attracting millions of fans, which placed book censorship in a new perspective. It was a different sensory experience to actually see real images rather than imagine and interpret them as readers. Reading a story in a book simply did not have the power to shock or corrupt a reader when compared to the dramatic visual effects a movie might have on a viewer. Other factors caused an increase in the mass popularity of books, such as the publication of inexpensive paperbacks and the existence of copyright laws that encouraged American authors and stopped the illegal reproduction of European books in America. A new generation of writers and publishers began printing and selling more realistic books. A change in American lifestyles and the introduction of new ideas and values followed the amazing technological advances, the freedom of women to vote and enter the workplace, and wider mobility due to the growth of automobile ownership. This changing sophistication of American culture was part of the groundswell that led to the changes in social attitudes and societal controls that weakened the strength of censorship.

Modern Times

In general, the latter half of the twentieth century brought an explosion of change in America's moral attitudes. Books once considered risqué were moved from locked cabinets to open library shelves. Our use of language reflects this change. Books once called "obscene" or "pornographic" are now called "classic." Swear words are more acceptable in public, and readers have become broad-minded about previously taboo, or forbidden, subjects. No longer are bad words or references to unwed pregnancy or adultery grounds by themselves for banning literature. In fact, legally, there must be a consideration of a book's overall literary or artistic merit for it to be considered inappropriate. The larger issues today involve the Internet and the tension between freedom of speech and concerns about protecting children from harmful material.

In the past half century, as the media in all of its forms has gained a great deal of freedom, there are those who would curb that freedom for the good of others. For many centuries, autocratic dictators or the church quieted heretics and dissenters who spoke against the status quo. This authoritarian censorship has almost disappeared in modern democracies. As organizations like vice societies emerged in America, interest groups began to carry the banner of censorship on behalf of their causes. In one sense, this represented a form of self-censorship, with voices rising out of the community itself in concern over certain issues. However, this presents a problem in a complex society.

30

Who has the right to decide what others can do? In a democracy where political power and public opinion shift from time to time, is there one standard that can be agreed on for the good of the entire society? Do we allow the strong voices of an interest group to dictate what the majority of citizens can do? Does the number of people who support an idea determine whether or not it is protected? Should the ideas of society be held captive by those who have stricter standards or more easily offended sensibilities than their fellow citizens?

It is naïve to believe that a perfect society would ever be completely free from censorship. The reality is that constraints on budgets and space drive decisions in the marketplace as well as in libraries and classrooms. People who buy materials make decisions on the basis of their personal and professional wisdom. One might consider selection and censorship to be close cousins and wonder where one ends and the other begins. Even in a democracy, there is a degree of governmental protection that holds

Types of Objectionable Speech

cursing, swearing—Words that are abusive, vulgar, or irreverent (also called profanity).

defamation—Speech intended to injure others (includes libel and slander).

lewd—Indecent; treating sexual matters in a vulgar way.

obscenity—Speech that is indecent or lewd.

pornography—Words or images intended to cause sexual arousal.

slurs—Terms that debase people in particular groups, such as racial or ethnic insults.

such subjects as child pornography unacceptable in a
reasonable society. Parents themselves have an obliga-
tion to protect their young children from vulgarity and
excessive violence. Often parents challenge books in
schools not because they believe them to be inherently
bad, but because they believe they are inappropriate for
a particular age group. In her Library of Congress lecture, L'Engle says,

> We all practice some form of censorship. I
> practiced it simply by the books I had in the
> house when my children were little.…
> Nobody said we were not allowed to have
> points of view. The exercise of personal taste
> is not the same thing as imposing personal
> opinion.[11]

Censorship and National Security

Security is an issue during times of national crisis, and
censorship is used by governments—including the U.S.
government—during wartime to ensure national safety
and security. During World War I, librarians conducted
programs for servicemen and removed objectionable
titles on the advice of the War Department.[12]
Censorship of both the outgoing and incoming mail
as well as the news coverage took place. Pacifist
publications or books that depicted the spirit of
America in poor light were frowned upon. In fact, the
vice societies, whose power had been waning, were
excited by the sudden national preoccupation with

morality during World War I. It seemed anti-American to focus on anything vulgar or inappropriate while servicemen were fighting for the cause of liberty. Propaganda is a form of communication that is carefully shaped to create the greatest influence. During all times of war, it is issued to boost support of government efforts. The American soldier is portrayed as a paragon of moral excellence as opposed to the obscene brutes who are the enemy.[13]

Any perceived threat to democracy or patriotism brings out the censors. One example occurred during World War I, when a person could be jailed for distributing pamphlets against the draft. A more dramatic event happened in the 1950s when Senator Joseph McCarthy led his infamous investigating committee on a massive hunt for Americans whom they suspected of being Communists or Communist sympathizers. Because America is a free country, some citizens chose to belong to the Communist party or supported its ideals. This was not illegal according to our Constitution. However, the committee interrogated government officials as well as artists, writers, actors, and others in the public eye, believing that any support of the Communist ideology was treasonous and un-American—and further believing that such supporters were most likely to be Soviet spies. Although books were not burned, intimidation censored voices as people were unwilling to speak out against McCarthy for fear of reprisal. Many people were under suspicion, and others lost their jobs or had to leave the country.

33

Some say a parallel situation exists today, when citizens are concerned about the Patriot Act, which was put into law following the attacks on the World Trade Center and the Pentagon on September 11, 2001. The Patriot Act gives the government the authority to access personal information on its citizens, such as their medical records or the books they buy or borrow from the library. Because this type of information has traditionally been considered personal and private, some people disagree with this part of the Patriot Act. They argue that allowing the U.S. government access to this information compromises American citizens' rights under the First Amendment. The U.S. government claims that a strong Patriot Act is necessary in order to protect the country against terrorists.

Special Interest Groups

Censorship reaches all parts of the political and religious spectrum. Some religious groups would prohibit publication of anything that is overtly sexual, improper, or counter to their strict beliefs. For them, society has gone too far with free expression. On the other hand, there are people who consider themselves to be more open-minded. Yet even as they disagree with others for their narrow framework, they themselves might seek to ban classics such as *Adventures of Huckleberry Finn* or *Uncle Tom's Cabin* for what they say is their outdated and racist portrayal of people of color, or *Little House in the Big Woods* for its stereotyped portrayals of Indians. Each group seems to have its own idea of what is appropriate based on their personal values. Their intention to ban materials can range from the protection of all society to placing limitations on what children can read or be instructed to read in schools.

Often particular interest groups object to a specific issue, as did the farmers in the agricultural community of Kern County, California, who were disturbed in the early 1940s by John Steinbeck's portrayal of a poor migrant family in *The Grapes of Wrath*. The Bible continues to be a controversial book. Various interest groups have attempted to remove it from such venues as comparative religion courses at the college level as well as from school libraries and public institutions. Censorship has become a confusion of private interests working to keep objectionable ideas away from the public and drawing on their own authority to decide what should or should not be available to others. It has become a free-for-all in the marketplace and the courtrooms of America.

Quoting a national survey on free expression in 1991, Robert Wyatt and David Neft report that free expression is in deep trouble because of the survey respondents' "inability to distinguish between what the law protects and what they dislike personally." They go on to say that Americans "only believe that they believe in free expression."[14] The report refers to the arena that has now become the stage for the greatest show of censorship—the protection of children. School libraries and the classrooms of America have become the battleground in the fight for ideas and how these ideas are communicated.

35

Chapter 3

Censorship in Schools and Libraries

Prior to the twentieth century, children were often seen as adults-in-training in need of strict rearing in order to teach them religious and moral principles. Although a few philosophers such as John Locke (1632–1704) and Jean-Jacques Rousseau (1712–1778) paid attention to how children matured and developed, it was not until the late nineteenth century and early twentieth century that child study became a fully recognized science. The first fiction authors did not write books specifically for children. Instead, early literature was written down in order to preserve the fables and legends of oral tradition. Myths explained the origins of the universe or the understanding of existence. They were also lessons for adults written as allegories or metaphors on life. We now consider works such as Charles Perrault's *Stories of Mother Goose*, written in 1697, and Grimm's fairy tales, published in the early 1800s, to be children's literature. However, they were not written for that purpose.

During the nineteenth-century Victorian period, the interest in child study led to a body of literature being produced by first-rate authors and illustrators specifically for children. Fantasies such as Lewis Carroll's *Alice's Adventures in Wonderland*, stories of adventure for boys such as Mark Twain's *The Adventures of Tom Sawyer*, and domestic stories for girls such as Louisa May Alcott's *Little Women* are a few examples of the best books published during that time.[1]

Literature in the Schools

The first schoolbooks used in America were developed in order to guide and teach religious and moral principles in addition to academic subjects. In 2006, *Wall Street Journal* columnist Cynthia Crossen wrote, "Tenets of Christianity were embedded in almost every lesson and book, including spelling, reading, history, grammar, arithmetic and science."[2] Students often attended one-room schools taught by a single teacher. In early years in America, only the sons of privileged families were sent to school. Later, as literacy spread through the country, largely based on ideas that more people should be able to read the Bible, both boys and girls attended school. However, was allowed to learn to read. Poorer children and slaves were excluded from formal schooling. In fact, teaching a slave to read was considered a crime. Although enrollment grew steadily over the years, it was not until after the early 1900s that the states passed compulsory attendance laws. Students from all socioeconomic groups now went to school. School attendance grew from 15 million to 75 million by the end of the twentieth century.[3]

This influx of a larger and more diverse student population caused schools to move away from the relatively homogeneous curriculum found in the earlier days of American education. Texts no longer included overtly religious content. Schools inherited the task of introducing American ideals to immigrants as well as socializing the student population through classes such as physical education and home economics. But even as new ideas about education developed in the first half of the century, very little contemporary American literature could be found in schools. Most English classes relied on British or nineteenth-century American works. In addition, books were expensive. In 1935 Britain's Penguin Books launched its first paperback book. Within thirty years, this new industry had made it economically possible to buy sets of books for school classrooms in America. Teachers could teach current literature and students could read the entire text instead of excerpts from an anthology.[4]

Compulsory education brought many children into the classroom who had previously been excluded. Court decisions in the 1950s mandated that students of different races be educated together. With the advent of the Education of All Handicapped Children Act in 1975, disabled children won the right to a free and appropriate public education under the law. Sensitive to diversity among the student populations, educators were challenged to meet the variety of interests and abilities. They also began to adopt a heightened sensitivity to inappropriate and outdated portrayals of gender and racial stereotypes in traditional textbooks.

Past generations of families adopted a "hands-off" attitude when it came to interfering in their children's education. One legacy of the controversial Vietnam War after the 1960s was a freedom to question authority. At the same time, publishers began issuing a new breed of books for children and young adults that were more realistic and dealt with a range of issues that had previously been taboo, such as poverty, race relations, divorce, and sexuality. As schools changed, new educational approaches seemed foreign and even threatening to many parents and grandparents, who

A teenager studies in a library. Throughout history, some have believed that young people need guidance about what they should read.

individually and in organized groups began to step up and voice their concerns.

Censorship has become the weapon of choice for those who have issues with the schools. Battles are waged on many fronts and by diverse groups across the political spectrum. Two groups that are especially vocal are those who seek to restore the values of the past and those who strive for a more inclusive future. Both sides have questions about what their children read and are concerned that the curriculum will shape their child's behavior. Their protests are directed at both the state and community level. Fundamentalist Christians want nothing in schools that violates their religious beliefs. More liberal groups are focused on what they see as stereotyping or negative portrayals of people because of their gender, race, ethnicity, or religion.

Textbooks

One battleground is the textbook industry. Textbooks and anthologies provide teachers with a wide spectrum of information in one publication making them economically feasible for school districts. Before the advent of the Internet and instant access to primary sources, these texts were often the main resource students were offered on a particular subject. Textbooks are usually adopted at the state level by review committees that are made up of a variety of people with particular concerns and points of view.

In 1961, Texans Mel and Norma Gabler became involved with textbook adoption because they were frustrated by their son's classroom materials. They were discouraged by what they perceived as the inaccuracy and moral laxness the books contained. They took their concerns to the state committee. Even though they had no educational credentials or college degrees, the Gablers became powerful proponents of change in the textbook industry. As an example of their efforts, one year the Gablers provided 659 pages of objections to twenty-eight state textbooks in literature and American history.[5] They were highly successful in challenging and removing books they felt were not worthy or appropriate for use in the schools.

Two groups that are especially vocal in the censorship debate are those who seek to restore the values of the past and those who strive for a more inclusive future.

Since Texas and California are the two largest purchasers of textbooks, their influence on publishers is felt throughout the country. It is financially unfeasible to issue different texts for smaller states. The Gablers' point of view is clearly stated on their Web site and includes their disagreement with the teaching of evolution and their preference for reading instruction based on phonics. They wish textbooks to include more examples of traditional gender roles and a conservative religious definition of marriage and family. Some critics suggest that people like the Gablers view school

41

materials as a means of passing on a cultural tradition circumscribed by white, Protestant, nineteenth-century values.[6]

The Gablers and their supporters are not the only interest group influencing textbooks. In her book *The Language Police*, Diane Ravitch writes about the bias and sensitivity reviews conducted by educational publishers. Although she says that these reviews are admirable in their intentions, she feels that they have evolved into a bizarre policy of censorship causing words, images, passages, and ideas to be deleted from texts, anthologies, and tests that go beyond reason. In fact, she worries that "the world may not be depicted as it is and as it was, but only as the guideline writers would like it to be."[7]

Ravitch is not the only writer who is concerned that it has become a national epidemic to exclude important subjects and historical events from our nation's textbooks in order to satisfy individual agendas. Dictionaries are under attack for containing "dirty words," historical events such as the Watergate scandal or the Holocaust are rewritten to put the nation in a more positive light, and anything that might be considered controversial, anti-American, non-Christian, or offensive to any particular group is omitted. Poet Myra Cohn Livingston tells about the time that textbook editors removed the word "matches" from a limerick she had written because, they said, children should not be encouraged to play with matches.[8]

42

Ravitch describes the myriad of pressure groups advocating for their own particular cause. Words and images as simple as dinosaur, slave, mouse, peanuts, cake, snowman, and America cause problems for certain groups. Any word that might offend someone is removed from the text, or bowdlerized. This term is named after a physician, Dr. Thomas Bowdler, and his sister, Henrietta Maria Bowdler, who cleaned up Shakespeare's works in the early 1800s by cutting out the parts "that contained sexual language, profanity, or irreverent references to God or Jesus."[9] Ravitch believes that textbooks have been bowdlerized to death. Since young people are exposed to television and the Internet, as well as other parts of the culture, she feels that such censorship creates two problems. "One is boredom because what is given is such pabulum, and the other is cynicism because [students] know that what they read in books has been sanitized … and is contrary to reality."[10]

Because the enormous textbook industry is driven by profit, publishers try to cater to critics in order to sell their books. When publishers are aware of concerns and expect strong reactions from interest groups, they pre-censor their books before publishing in order to escape controversy. Some believe that this form of censorship is more dangerous than direct challenges to individual books. It is easier to respond to a direct challenge than to a decision that has been made before the book is even published.

At the same time that students are expected to become critical and divergent thinkers in a pluralistic and democratic society, textbooks adopted after extensive review in order to meet all guidelines deny students exposure to other voices and ideas, multiple interpretations of history, and the opportunity to grapple with difficult issues and learn from the mistakes of the past. Students have the right to educational experiences that promote inquiry, critical thinking, and diversity in thought and expression, according to the National Council of Teachers of English. The denial or restriction of this right is an infringement of intellectual freedom.[11] Barbara Cohen is an author whose book *Molly's Pilgrim* was originally shorn of all mention of Jews, Sukkos (a Jewish holiday), God, and the Bible when it was adapted for a textbook. Only references to Jews and Sukkos were restored after negotiations. The publisher did not want the book to be offensive to any one group, causing it to lose income. Ravitch quotes Cohen as saying, "Censorship in this country is widespread, subtle, and surprising. It is not inflicted on us by the government. It doesn't need to be—we inflict it on ouselves."[12]

Books, Reading, and Censorship

L'Engle reports two places where a British publisher made changes to her stories in order to make them more "decent" for young readers. When *A Ring of Endless Light* was reissued in England, it was considered inappropriate for fifteen-year-old Vicky Austin to hold her eighteen-year-old brother's hand at a funeral. In *The*

Moon by Night, Vicky goes to her aunt and uncle's house after a traumatic evening. Although her uncle has been in bed, the publisher wanted him fully dressed rather than in his pajamas as the scene was written.[13] One famous recent example travels the opposite way across the ocean when Scholastic Books altered the Harry Potter novels to make the language more accessible to American children. Among the many changes were the title of the first book (from *The Philosopher's Stone* to *The Sorcerer's Stone*); in addition, the word "mummy" became "mommy" and "cinema" became "movies." There is a legitimate controversy among educators about whether it is best to change the words so that children can better understand the text or whether American children should be given an opportunity to reach out of their comfort zone in order to learn more about British culture from their reading.

Patricia Zettner wrote a story entitled "A Perfect Day for Ice Cream" that appeared in *Seventeen* magazine. However, when it was selected for publication in a junior high literature anthology, the name was changed to "A Perfect Day," and references to chili burgers, pizza, and ice cream were removed to comply with California's ban on junk food.[14] One of the concerns authors have when something like this happens is that publishers do not acknowledge deletions in the text by the addition of punctuation to show the omission. Nor do they always get permission for changes from writers. (This is especially interesting in light of the fact that

45

students are taught that this practice is unethical in their writing.)

Between 1990 and 2000 there were 6,364 direct challenges to books reported or recorded by the Office for Intellectual Freedom of the American Library Association and the Freedom to Read Foundation. Larger libraries are most likely to receive challenges due to the size of their collections. School libraries are more vulnerable than public libraries, which also serve adults and have fewer regulations than public schools.[15] During the 1990s, three quarters of the challenges were to remove materials from schoolrooms or school libraries, while one quarter of the challenges were made against materials at the public libraries. Most challenges are brought by parents.[16] A challenge is a formal, written complaint on file that comes from a person or a group who objects to materials in print and asks that they be removed or restricted from use. Approximately one third of challenges result in books being banned from the classroom or library shelves.

There are some curiosities about book challenges. Only a fraction of them get reported to organizations such as the American Library Association that keep statistics. Statistics that are compiled do not include the great percentage of books that are suppressed at the district or school level by administrators, principals, teachers, or librarians who will not order the books because they might be controversial. Contemporary fiction for young adults is by far the most challenged material in schools, for it often deals with subjects especially interesting to teens such as dating, sex, family problems, illness, death, or other realistic topics. Interestingly, the same authors and books are challenged again and again, while others appear to be ignored. For instance, attempts to ban L'Engle's *A Wrinkle in Time* have consistently put her on the lists of the most challenged authors even though she wrote the novel in 1962. *Many Waters* is the only other book in her time travel series that has been challenged, even though all the books include the same elements that people object to in *A Wrinkle in Time*. The final irony is that when a book appears on a censored list, it becomes "forbidden fruit" for students. That fact alone boosts its popularity. Sales rise in relationship to the amount of notoriety a book receives. This means that authors, who are not appreciated by those who would ban their books, sell more of them.

Silent censorship, according to authors Dave Jenkinson and Pat Bolger in their article "Censorship," is the attempt to remove materials from the system without the fanfare that accompanies a direct challenge. Instead, "light-fingered" censors simply steal the offending material.[17] Bette Keller, an elementary school librarian in Washington State, tells about the time in the early 1990s that she and her assistant were taking inventory. They realized that a number of books were missing and checked them against the card catalog. They discovered that every book on witches had been stolen from the collection. Because of the difficulty that must have been involved in cross-checking each book with the card catalog and taking them one by one to escape detection, they decided that the thefts had been committed by an adult rather than a student.[18] In the March 5, 2007, *Bellingham Herald*, syndicated columnist Leonard Pitts, Jr., writes about a woman acting on behalf of the Concerned Cuban Parents Committee who stole a book from a Miami elementary school library because "she felt it painted an inaccurately rosy picture of life in Cuba." According to the article, she checked out the book and announced that she had no intention of returning it. Pitts had a copy of the missing book shipped back to the library at his own expense, as did a group called Friends of Cuban Libraries. He asks, "Do we all get to remove from the library any book that hurts our feelings? Pretty soon you wouldn't have a library—just a room full of empty shelves."[19]

At times, censorship issues seem to be humorous. The Tarzan stories were banned because he and Jane could not find a minister in the jungle to marry them.[20] *The Rabbits' Wedding* was taken off of the open shelves in the Alabama public library in 1959 because a black rabbit was marrying a white rabbit.[21] Two California school districts banned *Little Red Riding Hood* because she took a bottle of wine to her grandmother,[22] and Robin Hood was labeled a Communist because he robbed the rich and gave to the poor.[23] All these books were contrary to some parents' belief system, and they did not want their children to read about them. As parents, they have the right to decide what their children

48

are exposed to. The larger issue is why parents would restrict other children from reading them as well.

According to a 2002 article in the *Washington Post*, book burning is still one method of censorship. In December 2001, a church pastor in Alamogordo, New Mexico, led about five hundred people in a ceremony where they tossed copies of J. K. Rowling's Harry Potter books, Tolkien novels, Shakespeare plays, magazines, and Ouija boards into a bonfire.[24] Harry Potter is a continual problem for censors because of the magic in the books and the disrespect Harry shows toward his uncle and aunt. Disrespect is also the problem many parents have with books like the popular and sassy *Captain Underpants* series, which appeals to young children. There is a parental fear that children will copy these antics and rebel against their family. One of the most popular and most censored children's authors, Judy Blume, writes about real issues that are meaningful to preteens, such as sexuality, which some parents consider taboo. L'Engle's *A Wrinkle in Time* is rejected because of her use of fantasy and telepathy as well as time travel. Even long-time classics such as *Huckleberry Finn, The Catcher in the Rye*, and *Black Beauty* cannot escape censorship. It seems that a book does not exist that is not offensive to someone.

Opponents of censorship sometimes question whether people actually read the books they wish to ban. Madeleine L'Engle tells about the time that a librarian told her that a woman had counted 7,432 dirty words in *The Catcher in the Rye*. But she told the librarian that she had not actually read the book, only counted the words.[25] Reading is a curious process that takes place solely within the reader's mind. Far from a passive activity, reading becomes a partnership between the author's words and the reader's imagination. It is possible for someone to "read in" different meanings or whatever their imagination supplies in a text. Often what one person reads in a text differs from what another person reads. Characters and scenery, for instance, might be imagined differently from one reader to the next. Fiction does not pretend to be true even when it is realistic. Fairy tales are often allegories, and larger truths are hidden beneath the words. If you go beneath the literal text and dig deeper to find new meanings, the surface of the story becomes less important. Harry Potter, it could be argued, actually treats his uncle rather well under the circumstances and only retaliates against his overt abuse. If not taken literally, the uncle's antics can be interpreted to show how ignorance and fear exist in the world.

The Freedom to Read

Academic freedom has been defined by several court cases in the past. In 1969, in *Tinker* v. *Des Moines Independent Community School District*, the Supreme Court decided in favor of a group of students who were expelled after they wore black armbands to school to protest the Vietnam War. The Court held that students "do not shed their constitutional rights at the school-house gate" and that the First Amendment protects public school students' rights to express political and social views.[26] In 1975, in *Island Trees* v. *Pico*, a school board repeatedly tried to remove books they believed were objectionable from a school library even after a review committee recommended that all but two be returned to the regular or restricted shelves. After years of appeal, the Supreme Court upheld the students' challenge by a 5 to 4 vote. Justice Brennan wrote:

> Local school boards may not remove books from school library shelves because they dislike the ideas contained in those books and seek by their removal to prescribe what shall be orthodox in politics, nationalism, religion, or other matters of opinion.[27]

And just one year later, in *Minarcini* v. *Strongsville City School District*, the U.S. Court of Appeals for the Sixth Circuit ruled against a school board who wished to ban materials from the library. "The removal of books from a school library is a ... serious burden upon the freedom of classroom discussion."[28] These are but a few of the many cases that echo the Supreme Court's proclamation. In 1967, in *Keyishian* v. *Board of Regents*, the U.S. Supreme Court declared: "Our nation is deeply committed to safeguarding academic freedom ... the classroom is peculiarly the 'marketplace of ideas.'" The Court then quoted an earlier case, *Sweezy* v. *New Hampshire*: "Teachers and students must always remain free to inquire, to study and to evaluate to gain new maturity and understanding otherwise our civilization will stagnate and die."[29]

Questions to Ponder

Several questions emerge from these concerns. Do the rights listed in the First Amendment apply to children? Do children have the freedom to read what they wish or to express their opinions, even if those opinions are unpopular or offend their parents or other adults? Certainly, parents have not only the right but also the responsibility to see that their children's education reflect their values. But does one parent have a right to decide what other parents' children should read or not read? How does society honor diversity while respecting each group's particular interests? Since the Constitution clearly provides for the separation of church and state, how can any group demand that school materials follow specific religious ideas? Should freedom of speech include any reasons for censorship within society? Should the concern for not offending any specific group prevent schoolchildren from being exposed to the great authors of the past? Do children's authors go too far with realism? Who sets the standard? These are questions that should be discussed by all who have a stake in public school education.

Chapter 4

Madeleine L'Engle: "Dare to Be Creative!"

On November 16, 1983, author Madeleine L'Engle gave an address entitled "Dare to Be Creative!" to a packed auditorium at the Library of Congress. As the National Children's Book Week speaker, she talked about the issue of censorship, a subject much on her mind because of her experiences. Any writer, she stated, assumes a great responsibility when his or her books are read by children who naturally are open and able to confront and grapple with difficult concepts.[1] Her book *A Wrinkle in Time* was originally rejected by all the major publishers because they did not believe that the book would sell or appeal to children. Before writing the novel, L'Engle had been absorbed in reading Einstein's theory of relativity and Planck's quantum theory. When she began writing, she combined those scientific ideas with fantasy to make her characters travel beyond ordinary time and space to save their imprisoned father on a distant planet. Although science fiction and fantasy were not completely new to historic literature, L'Engle joined writers such as J.R.R. Tolkien, C. S. Lewis, and Ursula LeGuin in a mid-twentieth century revival of the genre.

A Newbery Winner

Madeleine L'Engle was a successful writer even before she wrote *A Wrinkle in Time*. She had six novels in print, which made the repeated rejections of *A Wrinkle in Time* so painful. L'Engle loved the book and believed that her story was special even if the editors who rejected it did not. Readers would soon agree with her. In less than a year after John Farrar of the firm of Farrar, Straus and Giroux took a chance and published the book, it won the coveted Newbery Medal, awarded annually to an American author who makes a distinguished contribution to American literature for children. A 2004 article in *The New Yorker* magazine reported that *A Wrinkle in Time* had more than 6 million paperback copies in circulation and annual sales of approximately fifteen thousand hardcover editions.[2]

L'Engle told her audience at the Library of Congress that she agrees with editors and publishers who exercise restraints when they refuse to publish books they consider pornographic, ethically prejudiced, or potentially damaging to children. She thinks it is appropriate to do so. She has said that we all practice some form of censorship. Every time we decide which book to buy with a limited budget, there are books we choose not to buy. "Nobody said we were not allowed to have points of view. The exercise of personal taste is not the same thing as imposing personal opinion."[3] However, she does express her concerns about people who apply their own moral criteria to the books in public and school libraries. She said, "The best children's books ask questions, and make the reader ask questions. And every new question is going to disturb someone's universe."[4] She also quoted Edward P. Morgan, an American journalist and broadcaster, who said: "A book is the only place in which you can examine a fragile thought without breaking it, or explore an explosive idea without fear it will go off in your face...."[5] She added:

> Perhaps people who read and write and have enough vocabulary to think with *are* universe disturbers. We need to have the vocabulary to question ourselves, and enough courage to disturb creatively, rather than destructively, even if it is going to make us uncomfortable or even hurt.[6]

Early Years

Madeleine L'Engle Camp was born November 29, 1918, in New York City shortly after the end of World War I. Her father, Charles Wadsworth Camp, was a writer; her mother, Madeleine Hall Barnett Camp, a talented pianist. Before the war, her father had been a foreign correspondent, and he and her mother had traveled extensively. After the war, he had an office in New York and continued to write for a living. Her parents had a wide circle of friends who were artists and musicians. L'Engle remembers her mother and father busily attending the theater or the opera or having people in for parties. Madeleine's parents had been married almost twenty years before she was born. Although they had longed for a baby, they were used to a style of life that did not include a child. Madeleine, an only child, was raised with a nanny and governess and spent most of her lonely childhood eating meals in her room and writing stories, drawing, learning to play the piano, and reading her favorite books. She talks about that time in her book, *Walking on Water: Reflections on Faith and Art*:

> I wrote stories because I was solitary, the only child in New York City with no easily available library where I could get books…. It was through story that I was able to make some small sense of the confusions and complications of life.[7]

Madeleine and her parents lived in an apartment near Central Park. She fondly remembers her beloved English nanny, Mary O'Connell. "Mrs. O" became a stabilizing influence on young Madeleine and indulged her against her mother's wishes by secretly hiding sugar in the bottom of her oatmeal bowl. Her nanny or parents read to her every day. She wrote her first story—about a little "grul"—when she was five years old and just learning to spell. Her father gave Madeleine her first typewriter when she was ten years old. Her favorite books were by the author Lucy Maud Montgomery, who is best known for her Anne of Green Gables stories. But Madeleine liked *Emily of New Moon* best and read it over and over. Emily, a kindred spirit to Madeleine, was also an only child who had difficulty in school and had an ailing father. Madeleine also read fairy tales and myths from different countries.

When Madeleine was six, she attended first grade at a private school. She was miserable during her early school years. She was awkward and not particularly athletic because of an illness as a toddler that left one leg shorter than the other. She felt that her teachers disliked her; she remembers them always finding fault with her. She gives an example of the time that she entered a poetry contest and won. Her teachers did not believe that she had written the poem herself, and they accused her of copying

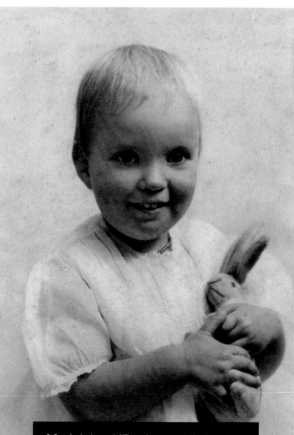

Madeleine L'Engle as a little girl. The author's lonely childhood was a theme in many of her books.

it. Madeleine's mother went to school carrying examples of the poems, novels, and stories she constantly wrote at home before the teachers would concede that perhaps she did deserve to win the prize. L'Engle remembers only a few early teachers who recognized her potential. One of them taught sixth grade at Todhunter School for girls in New York City. Her name was Margaret Clapp. It was her first year of teaching, and she was Madeleine's homeroom teacher. Clapp later became the president of Wellesley College.

> *Madeleine spent most of her lonely childhood eating meals in her room and writing stories, drawing, learning to play the piano, and reading her favorite books.*

Madeleine's parents left the United States and went to live in Switzerland when she was twelve. Her parents had always disagreed about how she should be raised and often used her as a battleground for their bickering. In Switzerland, her mother wanted her to attend the local French school and her father disagreed because he thought the education would be inferior. After a summer in the French Alps, her father got his way. They decided she would go to boarding school. Madeleine remembers that they took her for a car ride and abruptly left her with the matron of the school before they drove away. Classes had been in session for a week before she arrived, which made her feel even more like an outsider. She hated the school day, which was regimented from morning to evening with little free time until bedtime. She looked forward to her holidays. In her book *Penguins and Golden Calves*, she describes a vacation in their small villa in Chamonix, almost empty of tourists during the Great Depression. People were ice-skating in the afternoon under stars in the black sky, since the town had only a few hours of sunlight in December. Madeleine did learn how to survive in the school, which at least had beautiful views of Lake Geneva and the French Alps. She was later to use her boarding school experiences as settings in the novels *And Both Were Young* and *The Small Rain*. Her holidays from school were not without stress. She could observe her parents' unhappiness during vacations. Her father suffered from depression and damaged lungs as an aftermath of the war. Her mother was miserable living so far away from the city and the theater and friends.

The Camps returned to the United States when Madeleine was about fifteen and moved to the family beach house in Florida to be with her paternal grand-mother, whom she called Dearma. Her high school years at another boarding school, Ashley Hall in South Carolina, were her most successful school experiences. She made friends and won prizes for her poetry, which was published in the school literary magazine. She also served as the magazine's editor. When Madeleine was seventeen years old, in her senior year at Ashley Hall, she received news that her father had pneumonia. The principal called her to the office and said she needed to

Madeleine at age fifteen. Madeleine's high school years in the United States were happier than boarding school in Switzerland had been.

go home. She remembers trying to read the novel *Jane Eyre* during the trip to Florida on the train. Her father died before she arrived. Shortly after his death, her mother sold the beach house and moved to an apartment in Jacksonville, Florida, where she lived for the rest of her life.

Madeleine knew little about death, except that she must be brave. Her father's death shook her world at a time when she was finally finding success with school and her peers. She said:

> Father's death caused me to ask questions for which I could find no answer, and I was living in a world which believed that all questions are answerable. I, too, believe that all questions are answerable, but not in scientific terms, or in the language of provable fact.[8]

Marriage and Family

L'Engle went to Smith College in Massachusetts, where she continued to win awards for her poetry and wrote plays for her fellow students to perform. By the time she graduated with academic honors, she had seen several of her stories published in small magazines. Because she had been an impressionable youngster with a rich interior life, as she grew older, L'Engle was able to draw on early impressions and experiences when she developed the characters in her stories. After graduation, she moved to New York with her college friends and headed for the theater, where she found acting work as an understudy. She met actor Hugh Franklin while they were rehearsing *The Cherry Orchard*, a play by Anton Chekhov. Vanguard Press published L'Engle's first novel, *The Small Rain*, in 1945, when she was twenty-seven years old. The following year was an exciting one for L'Engle. She married Franklin, who was then working with the famous actress Ethel Barrymore, and her second novel, *Ilsa*, was published.

At the time her first writing was published, she chose to use her baptismal name, Madeleine L'Engle, instead of her father's surname, Camp. Later, she would make a decision to keep her professional name, L'Engle, rather than change it to her married name, Franklin.

Although both Madeleine and Hugh were New Yorkers at heart, they left the city with their five-year-old daughter, Josephine, in 1952 and moved to an old farmhouse they named Crosswicks in Goshen, Connecticut. Their son, Bion, was born soon after the move. In 1956, their daughter Maria came to them when she was seven years old, after both her parents, close friends of Madeleine and Hugh, tragically died within a year of each other.

In Connecticut, Hugh tried his hand at running a small general store in Goshen, and Madeleine continued writing while raising her children. The Franklins attended the local Congregational Church, where they made lifelong friends, but the Connecticut years were hard on the family. Trying to combine her writing career with raising children and owning a business, receiving a series of rejection slips for her work, and tragic events such as the death of Maria's parents made L'Engle's life difficult and sad at times. Almost a decade passed in which she wrote constantly but could get little published. Another rejection slip on her fortieth birthday caused her such frustration and lack of faith in herself that she was ready to cover her typewriter and give up writing altogether. However, in the midst of her misery, she found herself formulating a book in her mind about failure. At her very core, she realized, she was a writer. She believed that she was a better wife and mother when she was writing. She realized then that she had to write even if she never got published again.

The Franklins missed living in the city and felt isolated from other artists. So in 1959 they moved back to New York City, where Hugh resumed his acting career. They kept Crosswicks as a summer home and weekend retreat. Before moving, the family took a ten-week camping trip across the United States. Not only did the road trip experiences provide the material for a future novel about the Austin family, *The Moon by Night*, but also the idea for the three colorful characters (Mrs Who, Mrs Whatsit, and Mrs Which) in *A Wrinkle in Time* came to L'Engle during that vacation.

In the next two years, both *Meet the Austins* and *A Wrinkle in Time* were published. Finally having two new books in stores and then winning the Newbery award in 1963 was a tremendous boost to L'Engle after a long period of struggling through doubts and rejections. It encouraged her to keep writing and publishing.

By 1966, L'Engle was working as a volunteer librarian at the Cathedral of St. John the Divine. Her children had left home. Josephine had married, Maria left for college, and Bion went to boarding school. This Episcopal cathedral was to take on great importance in her life; not only did she work there for many years, but she also used it as a setting in two of her novels, *A Severed Wasp* and *The Young Unicorns*. She made one of her greatest friends there: Canon Nason Edward West. He was the model for Canon Tallis, one of the most colorful characters in several of her fiction books.

Madeleine L'Engle and Hugh Franklin, shortly after their marriage in 1946. The demands of raising three children did not keep L'Engle from her writing.

Hugh Franklin continued his successful acting career. From 1971 to 1983 he played his most famous role, that of Dr. Charles Tyler in the popular daytime television series *All My Children*. In 1985, Madeleine and Hugh traveled to Egypt as goodwill ambassadors for the U.S. Information Agency. They were such a popular team that they were also invited to tour China together. They performed joint readings for audiences.

Shortly after the tour, Hugh was diagnosed with cancer. He died in 1986. Two years later, L'Engle published *Two-Part Invention: The Story of a Marriage*, a journal that chronicled their life together and her thoughts about his illness and death.

Awards and Honors

After returning to New York and winning the Newbery Medal, L'Engle published a huge array of work that ranges from novels to essays, poetry, memoirs, picture books, and articles for all age groups and interest levels. She won numerous awards and was granted honorary doctoral degrees from a dozen institutions. She received over one hundred letters a week from her readers. She continued her work as volunteer librarian and writer-in-residence at the cathedral while she traveled extensively, giving seminars and workshops in schools and universities, speaking from pulpits and podiums across the continent and abroad.

In the introduction to her book *Madeleine L'Engle Herself: Reflections on a Writing Life*, Carole F. Chase says that L'Engle was known for creating a spirit of community, intellectual rigor, and spiritual renewal among those who attended her workshops.[9] For many years, she held a New York writers' workshop one night a week for six weeks. After each workshop ended, the groups stayed together and continued to meet regularly. They tried an annual reunion with the author until it got so large that it included hundreds of past students who had become her friends. She liked to do the writers' workshops. She said that they kept her technique fresh and offered young writers something that she, herself, would have liked when she began to write.[10] In 1975, L'Engle was invited to archive her papers and manuscripts for posterity in the Buswell Memorial Library at Wheaton College in Illinois.[11]

On a trip to San Diego in 1991, Madeleine L'Engle was severely injured in an automobile accident and was laid up in the hospital far away from family and friends. All her vital organs had been lacerated, and much of her body was bruised. In a book written after her accident, *The Rock That Is Higher: Story as Truth*, she says, "It is faith that helps my grief to be creative, not destructive. It is faith that kept me going through the pain at the very portals of death and pulled me ... back into life and whatever work still lies ahead."[12]

In an anthology of writings about L'Engle put together for her eightieth birthday by her friend Luci Shaw, Donald R. Hettinga wrote that we should understand L'Engle's critics who take her books seriously, because books do have the power to change people's lives. He said that Madeleine L'Engle "gives us books that show us something about the nature of the universe as well as something about the nature of God in relation to that universe."[13] When L'Engle was asked if her Christianity affects her stories, she replied that her stories affect her Christianity. They "restore me, shake me by the scruff of the neck, and pull this straying sinner into an awed faith."[14]

In 1998, L'Engle was awarded the Margaret A. Edwards Award for her lifetime contribution to young adult literature. It was the thirty-fifth anniversary of her winning the Newbery Medal. In 2004, the author was presented with the National Humanities Medal by President George W. Bush "for her talent as a writer on spirituality and art and for her wonderful novels for young people. Her works inspire the imagination and reflect the creative spirit of America."[15] Because of L'Engle's ill health, her granddaughter Charlotte Jones accepted the award on her behalf.

Chapter 5

The Storyteller: L'Engle's Characters and Themes

In an article in *The New Yorker* magazine, Cynthia Zarin writes that she read *A Wrinkle in Time* as a child. She then reread it every year. As an adult, she says, she is reading it to her children. Along with other books by L'Engle, it "influenced how I thought about religion and politics, about physics and mystery, and how I imagined what family life could be."[1] She says that when she was in college, a friend commented, "There are really two kinds of girls. Those who read Madeleine L'Engle when they were small, and those who didn't."[2] Writer Anne Lamott describes a time she was reading a book that had a profound affect upon her in her publication *Grace (Eventually): Thoughts on Faith*:

> I felt the way I had felt reading *A Wrinkle in Time* at eight … whenever a book had offered me a box with a treasure inside. It was what flooded out in the quiet, intimate relationship between me and the writer; the treasure of me.[3]

Although L'Engle's strong protagonists are role models for many female readers, her work also appeals to males. Jeffrey Bezos, the founder of Amazon.com and *Time* magazine's "Person of the Year" for 1999, remembers loving *A Wrinkle in Time* as a fourth grader.[4] In a paper entitled "Bridging to Infinity" that professor Mike Pinter of Belmont University presented to his faculty colleagues in 1997, he says, "L'Engle reminds me of the wonderful mystery that surrounds what I'm doing. There's a point where logic leaves off and I'm left staring at this beautiful and exciting concept of infinity

"There are really two kinds of girls. Those who read Madeleine L'Engle when they were small, and those who didn't."

with my very finite mind."[5] These kinds of statements are testimonies to her influence and to the strong impact that her writing has on readers. Her works provide entertainment and inspiration to millions of readers around the world. What is special about her writing, and why is it so popular?

The Storyteller

Madeleine L'Engle is first and foremost a storyteller. Whether she is weaving fantasy or other types of fiction, she draws her readers into the worlds she creates and offers them an opportunity to reflect on their own lives. Readers may find themselves transported to a farmhouse in Connecticut, to an island off the

69

coast of Portugal, to imagined distant planets, or to the time of Noah. Wherever they may find themselves, they recognize and relate to L'Engle's characters because they face familiar human predicaments. L'Engle says: "Story is the best way to address truth, to address the really important things. Using your rational mind will take you only so far."[6]

L'Engle has trouble understanding people who fail to see that story can be a vehicle for a deeper truth. She cites many authors who have used fairy tales and science fiction as an impetus to stir the imagination, noting:

> A story, instead of taking a child away from real life, prepares him [or her] to live in real life with courage and expectancy. A child denied imaginative literature is likely to have more difficulty understanding cellular biology or post-Newtonian physics than the child whose imagination has been stretched by fantasy and science fiction.[7]

Madeleine L'Engle once told her mother that she was grateful for her unique childhood because it gave her material for many of her books. She talks about this in *Madeleine L'Engle: Star*Gazer,* a documentary film made in 1990. "As I look back on my childhood and most of my life, it is apparent to me that the things that seem to be the most negative were the most important in forming me as a writer, and a woman, and a human being."[8] L'Engle believes that writers must write for themselves, out of their own need. Otherwise, stories lack integrity. But if a story is honest, it will have the ring of the truth and will appeal to others who seek truth in the books they read.[9] L'Engle's ability to write about the questions of life that she finds important binds her to readers of all ages. She shows her characters dealing with complex relationships, making difficult choices, asking questions about existence, and living in imperfect communities of family and friends. Even when she is writing fantasy, she grounds the experience for her characters in real day-to-day details. In *A Wrinkle in Time*, the main characters, Meg and her brother Charles Wallace, are able to travel through time and space. But they have everyday problems, too. Young readers do not need magical powers to relate to their concerns about poor grades, an absent father, or the peers who dislike them. These fears are understood by children everywhere.

L'Engle's books are placed by her publisher and libraries into categories—children's books, young adult books, adult fiction, and nonfiction—though she believes that good stories go beyond a narrow framework and can be read by anyone, of any age, anywhere. She has great respect for children and does not believe that children's books are books too simplistic for adults. When asked why some of her books are considered children's literature, she says one reason might be the age of the protagonist. She has written that "a children's book is any book a child will read."[10]

L'Engle has great faith in children's ability to understand important concepts. She also believes that there is no subject in art that is, in itself, taboo, either for children or adults. What matters, according to L'Engle, is the way a subject is handled. Often children see things that grown-ups miss because adults have lost their ability to approach the world with fresh eyes. *Meet the Austins* was first rejected because it begins with a death, and *A Wrinkle in Time* was rejected because it deals with the problem of evil. L'Engle responds:

> One of the objections to the book, other than it was too difficult, was that it deals too overtly with evil and that children should not know about evil. Believe me, children know about evil. The best thing we can do is to give them a light against darkness, not to pretend it isn't there.[11]

The popularity of her books shows that L'Engle's belief that children would respond to serious issues was well founded.

Characters and Themes

L'Engle's fictional characters are shaped by her own life experiences and her vast imagination. They are born out of her subconscious, and she claims that she cannot always "control" the people in her books. Sometimes they just appear, much to her surprise. A character will do something that she had not originally planned when plotting her book. L'Engle says:

72

An imaginary character is not limited; he does and says all kinds of things I don't expect, and often don't want.... the character is always right ... whether we know it or not ... we draw constantly from our subconscious minds.[12]

When she was writing *The Arm of the Starfish*, the character Joshua suddenly came to her. She had to rewrite many pages of the novel to make him part of the plot. However, she could not refuse to rewrite because it was an inconvenience. She believed that Joshua had appeared and become a real person to her. As a writer, she felt forced to acknowledge his presence and make room for him in the story. When she read the chapter in which Joshua is killed to her son, Bion, he got very angry with her and wanted her to change it. It was difficult to explain to a ten-year-old why his mother as the writer could not change the story just to please him or make things better. She writes that it took many years for Bion to "understand that the artist cannot change the work at whim, but can only listen, look, wait, and set down what is revealed."[13]

Perhaps because of her early experiences as a single child reared in part by servants and in boarding schools, family is a consistent theme that recurs in L'Engle's work. Her earlier works often mirror her own loneliness within her family and her feelings of separation from her parents. Her children's series all portray loving and close families. The Murry family from *A Wrinkle in Time*, the O'Keefes of *The Arm of the Starfish*, and the Austin family of *Meet the Austins* all love and care deeply for each other. This is shown clearly in *A Wrinkle in Time*, when Meg is able to save her brother from the clutches of evil only through the love she has for him. But each family also extends their love to others beyond the immediate family. In *Meet the Austins*, Maggie comes to live with the family after her father dies. In *A Ring of Endless Light*, the Austins travel to the island home of their Grandfather Eaton to be with him while he is dying of leukemia. L'Engle's novels include close friends who support the families, such as Canon Tallis, who reaches out to both the Austins and the O'Keefes in times of need. It might be fair to say that L'Engle portrays the families she wished she had or those she hoped to create for herself in real life.

It is no surprise that Calvin reads the book of Genesis to Charles Wallace as a bedtime story in *A Wrinkle in Time*. L'Engle weaves religion into all her writing. Sometimes her faith is the overt subject of a book, and other times it is revealed in the conversation of the characters. Her novels and poems are full of biblical references and quotes. She has written picture books based on Bible stories and novels such as *Many Waters*, which retells the story of Noah's ark. Her biblical accounts often add elements that deviate from the traditional story, which disconcerts some readers. Carole F. Chase writes in *Madeleine L'Engle, Suncatcher* that L'Engle uses her vast imagination to "express deep universal principles [of the story] without being factual." She says, "L'Engle believes in what she calls 'the limited realm of literalism.'"[14] L'Engle's religious beliefs and her faith appear in her nonfiction books. Chase reports that L'Engle believes we "are question-asking beings who … need myths, symbols, metaphors, icons, and stories to help us understand our questions and the meaning of our existence."[15]

L'Engle's playfulness with language can be seen with her choice of a fictional name for Canon West in her novels. Canon Tallis is a

L'Engle reads to her granddaughters Lena (on right) and Charlotte. Her children's books portrayed close, loving families.

perfect example of her creativity and sense of humor. L'Engle, a pianist and music lover, named Canon Tallis after the composer Thomas Tallis, whose most famous work is known as the "Tallis Canon." The word *canon* can mean both a musical form (like a round) or a clergyman. She simply made the switch from the music, Tallis Canon, to the clergyman, Canon Tallis. To make it even more delightful, she actually calls him Canon Tom in her novels.

Published Works

L'Engle's first published novel, *The Small Rain*, is the story of Katherine Forrester, a lonely young woman who attended boarding school and was left out of her musical parents' lives. *Ilsa, And Both Were Young*, and *Camilla Dickinson* followed within the next six years. (The last book was revised and reissued in 1965 under the title *Camilla*.) It is interesting that L'Engle brings back Katherine Forrester as a seventy-year-old retired concert pianist in the novel *A Severed Wasp*, published thirty-seven years after *The Small Rain*. She does the same thing to the character Camilla Dickinson, who reappears in a novel written forty-five years later, *A Live Coal in the Sea*. L'Engle agrees that once she meets her characters, she does not like to let them out of her life.

These semiautobiographical "coming-of-age" novels show the young L'Engle writing about what she knows best. All have young women protagonists who are either alienated from their parents or have a parent that has tragically died. They share common themes: being sent away to boarding school, feeling awkward, trying to grow up and find one's place in the world, and searching for love and meaningful relationships. A previously written novel, *The Joys of Love*, is scheduled to be published in the spring of 2008.

Tracking the story series published by Madeleine L'Engle can be complicated, since her books were not always written in order, and sometimes many years would pass before another would be added to a series. For instance, the original Time Trilogy about the Murry

76

family included *A Wrinkle in Time, A Wind in the Door*, and *A Swiftly Tilting Planet*. However, it became a quartet with the addition of *Many Waters*. The entire series was written over twenty-five years, with various other books published in between. Can you imagine Harry Potter fans having to wait twenty-five years to see what happens in the next installment? Just like the *Star Wars* films, the L'Engle series are sometimes written in unusual chronological order. *Many Waters* was the last to be written, but it comes third in the series, while the Murry children are still in school. In *A Swiftly Tilting Planet*, Meg is grown, and she and her husband, Calvin O'Keefe, are expecting a child. Meg, Calvin, and their offspring appear in four separate novels. Their daughter Polly has a fantasy adventure in *An Acceptable Time*, published three years after *Many Waters*. She visits her mother's parents, the Murrys, and travels back in time, adding yet another fantasy novel to the Time series. In May 2007, Square Fish (an imprint of Farrar, Strauss and Giroux) reissued all five of these books bundled together in a quintet.

The Austin family appears in eight novels. Often characters overlap with the separate series. Zach Gray, for instance, is boyfriend to both Vicky Austin and Polly O'Keefe, protagonists from two unrelated novels. Adam Eddington and Canon Tallis make appearances with both the O'Keefes and the Austins. Suzy from the Austin family is in *A Severed Wasp* with Katherine Forrester from the first published novel, *The Small Rain*.

If Madeleine L'Engle had written only her popular fiction, she would have had a long and successful professional career. But these works by no means define the writer. They add up to slightly half of her publications. Four of her most popular works are based on the daily journals she kept over the years. In *A Circle of Quiet*, she talks about her children and living at Crosswicks. *The Summer of the Great-Grandmother* recalls her mother and the family before her mother's death, *The Irrational Season* is filled with her reflections on life and faith, and the final book in the series, *Two-Part Invention: The Story of a Marriage*, is a moving account of her marriage and her husband's death. These Crosswicks Journals, as they are known, give her readers an opportunity to hear L'Engle reflect on her books and her life in her own words.

Madeleine L'Engle has written several books that writer Carole F. Chase calls her "personal reflections on scripture."[16] Some of them are biblical picture books for children. In *The Glorious Impossible*, L'Engle tells the life of Jesus illustrated by the magnificent paintings of Giotto. *Ladder of Angels* uses children's art from around the world to illustrate stories from the Bible. *And It Was Good: Reflections on Beginnings, A Stone for a Pillow: Journeys with Jacob*, and *Sold Into Egypt: Joseph's Journey into Human Being* make up the Genesis Trilogy; these are reflections on the first book of the Bible. *The Rock That Is Higher: Story as Truth* includes L'Engle's reflections following her serious car accident in San Diego.

Penguins and Golden Calves: Icons and Idols is an account of her trip with Bion and his wife, Laurie, to Antarctica in 1992. These books, along with books of prayers and poetry, are a sampling of Madeleine L'Engle's vast collection of works.

The Art of Writing

Madeleine L'Engle has been asked numerous times how she can write daily if she travels so often to conferences, workshops, and public appearances. She reports that while in her Swiss boarding school she learned to write anywhere, so she writes in airports, planes, hotel rooms, and wherever she is at the moment. She wrote her first two novels in her dressing room at the theater while waiting for her entrances on stage. She still keeps a journal, and has long since given up her first type-writer for a computer. She says that writing is a solitary business, as the writer withdraws from the world and attempts to put down what is "crying to be written." She says: "We write alone, but not in isolation … out of our responses to what is happening to us and to the world in which we live."[17] She is respectful of her readers and says that they often underestimate their importance. Reading is not passive like watching TV, but is cocreative with the writer. According to L'Engle: "In reading we must become creators—imagining setting, visualizing characters, seeing facial expressions, hearing inflections of voices. The author and the reader 'know' each other; they meet on the bridge of words."[18]

Much of what L'Engle writes about reflects her personal experiences. Her characters in *The Arm of the Starfish* stayed in the same hotel room in Madrid that L'Engle had stayed in when she traveled to Spain.[19] She visited Antarctica; the character Vicky Austin followed two years later in *Troubling a Star*. L'Engle wrote about the Austin family's camping trip across America in *The Moon by Night* four years after her family took the same trip. The settings in L'Engle's real world are often found in the settings to her novels, from the house at Crosswicks to her grandmother's beach cottage. Experiences that L'Engle had as a child creep into stories, tales of her relatives show up in her fiction, and her children and friends appear as models for her characters. L'Engle herself has admitted that she is her protagonists. She says, "I don't think we can write about any character that doesn't, to some extent, come out of our own selves, including more evil characters."[20] Because Madeleine L'Engle has written so much about herself and her family in her nonfiction books, one can see her life reflected in situations and characters in much of her fiction.

Cynthia Zarin, in her *New Yorker* article, reported that some of L'Engle's relatives suggest that her nonfiction stretches the truth. Madeleine L'Engle wrote, "My husband says … that by the time I've finished a book I have no idea what in it is fabrication and what is actuality … not only for novels but for most of my life."[21] Just as her fiction has a "ring of truth," perhaps her nonfiction has the ring of a good story.

Chapter 6

A Wrinkle in Time

Madeleine L'Engle's most popular novel has consistently been high on the lists of books that are widely assigned and also widely challenged in classrooms and school libraries. The primary reason for this is inherent in the genre—the magic that the characters encounter is exciting to young readers and of concern to some parents. *A Wrinkle in Time* is L'Engle's most famous novel and the most censored.

The Murry Family and Friends

A Wrinkle in Time begins with the familiar line "It was a dark and stormy night," used by Snoopy in the comic strip *Peanuts* whenever he began to write his novel.[1] The book introduces the Murry family. The eldest child, Meg, is an awkward, underachieving high school student who is talented in math and science. She is critical of her looks—her mouse-brown hair and teeth covered with braces—especially when she compares herself to her brilliant and beautiful mother, who has doctoral degrees in biology and bacteriology. Meg's ten-year-old twin brothers, Sandy and Dennys are good athletes and popular students. Her youngest brother, Charles Wallace, is five years old. He has telepathic powers and is very intelligent, although people assume he is somewhat retarded because he rarely speaks. The Murry children are worried about their father, an astrophysicist, who is on a top-secret mission and has been out of communication for a year. In Chapter 1, Charles Wallace, Meg, and their mother meet in the kitchen for a late-night snack when a curiously clad visitor named Mrs Whatsit arrives. Charles Wallace recognizes her as the lady who is living in an old haunted house in the woods. There is something strange about Mrs Whatsit, and she shocks Mrs. Murry with her assurance that "there is such thing as a tesseract."[2] This term refers to the important research that Mr. Murry was doing before he disappeared.

The following day, while walking their dog Fortinbras, Charles Wallace and Meg meet up with an older boy from Meg's school named Calvin O'Keefe who claims he was driven to the same spot in the woods by a strong compulsion. Surprisingly, Charles Wallace talks freely to Calvin, and they create an instant bond. He and Meg take the young man to the house in the woods to meet Mrs Whatsit. Instead they find her friend, Mrs Who, another strange lady who peppers her speech with pithy quotes in foreign languages. Mrs Who warns them to prepare because "it's getting near time."[3] When the children invite Calvin home for dinner, he says, "I've never even seen your house, and I have the funniest feeling that for the first time in my life I'm going home."[4] Later in the evening, Calvin and Meg go outside for a stroll. Charles Wallace finds them to say that it is time to go. He is not sure where, but he thinks they are going to find their father. Mrs Whatsit and Mrs Who appear and with them a third stranger, Mrs Which, who speaks in a strange but authoritative voice and does not always materialize completely.

Already in these first three chapters, curious incidents mark this book as one that will interweave magic and realism, science and the otherworldly into a fascinating and unpredictable story. Each child faces difficulties. Meg, like many teenagers, is self-critical and hates school. Charles Wallace is uncomfortable in public, and Calvin is popular at school but battles a difficult home life. The missing father introduces an element of mystery. Three very odd and quirky women appear to take the children on a journey to find their father. One claims to be a billion years old. Another startles Mrs. Murry by her knowledge of the curious tesseract. The third never fully materializes. The introduction of the three women moves the readers out of the realm of the literal into that of the imagination. L'Engle heightens this by purposely using a British style of punctuation. She drops the periods when writing about her magical characters such as Mrs Who, Mrs Whatsit and Mrs Which, so they will look unusual and mysterious. She adds the periods to more down-to-earth people such as Mr. and Mrs. Murry. This introduction of magic and the otherworldly will become the basis of one criticism leveled at the novel by parents and religious groups who believe that L'Engle is introducing inappropriate subjects to children.

Off Into Space

In the next few chapters, Mrs Whatsit, Mrs Who, and Mrs Which whisk the children away to the planet Uriel. Their method of travel is through the fifth dimension, or the tesseract, which provides a shortcut, or a "wrinkle," through time and space. Mrs Who illustrates the tesseract by stretching a length of her skirt taut between two fingers then decreasing the length by bringing the ends together until they meet. It is the path across the wrinkle that cuts off the long distance.

The children find themselves in an ethereal grassy, flower-adorned field that has a wonderful fragrance. Meg feels a great peace that is short-lived when Mrs Whatsit transforms into a large, magnificent, winged creature and takes the children on a flight to the summit of the mountains. Burying their faces in flowers so they can breathe in the thin atmosphere, they are shown a scary, dark shadow on the horizon that blots out the stars. They have no doubt that it is something very evil, and it is where they will find their father.

The party arrives at a gray and barren planet in Orion's belt. They are taken to meet a character called the Happy Medium, who uses her crystal ball to show them that the evil shadow also covers their beloved earth. They learn that darkness has been fought all over the cosmos for centuries by all the great religious and secular leaders of the world. Mrs Whatsit reveals that she, herself, gave up her life as a star in a battle with the dark Thing. The children are to be sent off into the darkness to search for their father on a planet called Camazotz. The three ladies send each of them off with wisdom and gifts. Mrs Whatsit strengthens Calvin's ability to communicate, she tells Meg that her faults will serve her well, and she can give only the resilience of his childhood to Charles Wallace. Mrs Who quotes words of Shakespeare to Calvin, gives her special glasses to Meg, and tells Charles that he does not know everything. Mrs Which commands them to go into town, be strong, and stay together. After tessering again into space, they find themselves in the capital city of Camazotz, where they observe identical houses and robotlike residents. They are told that the city is the home of "IT." With fear and trepidation, they head for "CENTRAL Central Intelligence" to find their father.

To readers of the twenty-first century familiar with *Star Wars*, a journey through time and space seems rather ordinary. We can imagine how Meg feels when she tessers through space, because we are used to fantasy images created by the technology of modern movies and television. But in 1962, the idea of traveling through time and space was an unusual component for a children's book.

L'Engle provides the children with three guardians who guide and protect them. They assure the children that the evil can be fought as it has been for ages. But they also indicate that evil is responsible for the earth's troubles. L'Engle's critics claim that the three women are witches. This most likely stems from Mrs Which's name and her antics. She materializes on Uriel dressed as a witch with a broomstick, much to the amusement of her two friends, who laugh hysterically at the sight. In Chapter 11, L'Engle makes it clear that the women are guardian angels and messengers of God. They were sent to assist Meg, Charles Wallace, and Calvin as their spiritual guides while allowing the children to take responsibility for their own actions.

L'Engle's most popular book, *A Wrinkle in Time*, is also her most challenged.

L'Engle's critics do not approve of the children visiting a medium, because that word can refer to a person who acts as a channel of communication between living people and the dead. They believe she is a sorceress. L'Engle is not using the word in this manner. In fact, she is having fun with her readers with another amusing play on words. In the first two chapters, Meg is told first by her mother and then her brothers that she has to find a happy medium in her life and not always go to extremes. During a lecture at Wheaton College, her critics brought up their concern about her using a medium in her novel, saying that "God abhors mediums, witchcraft, magic and the like."[5] L'Engle replied, "I didn't think of her as being a medium! She's a character who was a happy medium."[6] This was not funny to her critics, who felt L'Engle was making fun of their concerns. Another example of L'Engle's playful use of language occurs in the name of the planet, Camazotz, which comes from a Mayan legend about a vampire bat.[7] This seems appropriate for a dark planet where the lifeblood of humans is metaphorically drained to turn them into robots.

Much like the Wizard of Oz's gifts to Dorothy and her friends, the gifts given to the children to take into danger are traits they already possess. By this, L'Engle shows that people have everything they need within themselves to fight the shadows of darkness and evil. These are portrayed with traditional symbols of light representing the good and darkness representing evil. L'Engle is clear in the novel that the consequence of being overcome by the darkness is the loss of individuality and uniqueness, to be replaced by the mindless horror of forever living like robots in a controlled society.

The Pulse of Evil

The story continues as the three brave but fearful children make their way through CENTRAL Central Intelligence until they reach a man with weird red glowing eyes sitting on a platform under a steady, pulsing light. He tells them telepathically that he has been waiting for them. As he tries to draw them into his power, they resist by reciting words to distract themselves. He orders a feast to be brought. Charles Wallace recognizes that the food is an illusion. Then Charles makes the fatal decision to give in to the man in order to figure out who he is and to save his father. In doing so, his individual personality disappears and he appears to be under the spell of the man on the platform.

Charles is ordered to take Meg and Calvin to their father, imprisoned in a transparent column inside a locked cell. Meg finds that Mrs Who's spectacles gain her access to the cell. She is able to free her father and clings to him for comfort. In order to stick together, Meg, Father, and Calvin follow the hypnotized Charles Wallace out of the building to meet the mysterious IT. Entering a domelike building with the same rhythmic pulsing that they saw as light and felt as a throb deep within their bodies, they discover that the evil IT is a quivering, disembodied brain that seizes and commands all. Recognizing they are all in grave danger of being taken over like Charles Wallace, Meg's father tells her to recite the periodic table of elements to keep her mind free from IT. Calvin urges Father to tesser them

88

away from the planet. They save themselves, but have to leave Charles Wallace behind.

L'Engle presents the ultimate evil as a brain with no heart or emotion to temper ideas. Speaking as IT's subject, Charles Wallace argues with Meg, telling her that in a perfect world no one suffers because the ill or deformed are annihilated. It is not murder, he says. IT decides who should live or die by how well they conform to his will. Misfits are expendable. Charles reminds her how she hates school because she feels so different. He suggests that differences create all the unhappiness and problems in the world. But Meg can see the error in his logic. She realizes that her faults are also her assets. Her stubbornness has allowed her to resist the evil IT because she is too angry to give in. L'Engle makes her point clearly: People who give up their uniqueness and their power to choose lose them-selves to those who would choose for them.

Charles Wallace falls prey to IT because he is so sure of himself. He believes he has the strength and will to resist. Pride and arrogance are his downfall, as Mrs Whatsit suggested they might be. Calvin is the hero when he urges Father to save Meg from IT by tessering them off the planet. The rhythmical pulse that beats throughout Camazotz, especially in the presence of IT, is a sign of tedium without relief. It is a reminder that without human variation and differences, life would be an unending monotony.

Meg Rescues Charles Wallace

Father, who has not perfected the art of tessering, lands them on a rusty, gray planet called Ixchel. Meg is frozen and cannot move. She is angry with her father because he left Charles Wallace in danger. They are soon rescued by strange-looking furry creatures, and Meg is healed by the loving care she receives from one she calls Aunt Beast. Calvin tells the creatures about Mrs Who, Mrs Which, and Mrs Whatsit, describing them as guardian angels or messengers of God; before the beasts can understand, the women appear.

L'Engle makes her point clearly: People who give up their uniqueness and their power to choose lose themselves to those who would choose for them.

Meg realizes that she must go to back to save Charles Wallace because she is closest to him. Before she can free her brother, she asks her father's forgiveness for her own anger and resentment toward him. Meg is physically healed by Aunt Beast and spiritually cleansed by her father's forgiveness. She is prepared to go into battle to rescue Charles Wallace. Mrs Whatsit sends Meg off with her love forever, and Mrs Who gives her words of wisdom about how God has chosen the weak to confound the mighty. Mrs Which delivers Meg to Camazotz and tells her that she has something that IT does not have—and it is her only weapon.

Meg finds Charles Wallace, who taunts her, saying that she has nothing that IT does not have. She soon realizes that love is what she has that IT does not have. Love is the one weapon that Meg has to overcome the evil IT, who has no heart. She tells Charles Wallace repeatedly that she loves him, which frees his mind from IT. As she does so, they are caught up in darkness and find themselves delivered safely home into the twins' vegetable garden. Mrs Whatsit, Mrs Who, and Mrs Which disappear with the wind.

The book is filled with biblical references. Calvin reads the book of *Genesis* as a bedtime story to Charles Wallace. On Uriel, the centaurlike beings sing a hymn of joy from Isaiah. Words from the New Testament books of First and Second Corinthians are spoken by both Aunt Beast on Ixchel and Mrs Who when they are addressing Meg. When Mrs Who tells Meg that God chooses the weak to confound the mighty, Carole Chase says that L'Engle is reminding her readers that "God's view of the value and importance of 'things' and people is different from that of humans."[8] L'Engle is also referring to the Christian belief that the Messiah came as a little baby to save the world. Madeleine L'Engle has commented that "sometimes small unimportant people, superficially, are the ones who are called on to do what needs to be done."[9]

Madeleine L'Engle's writing has been praised for its strong female protagonists. Meg is no exception. Astronaut Janice Voss took *A Wrinkle in Time* along on her space mission because it had inspired her to become an astronaut even before women could qualify for the program.[10] Meg has all of the anxiousness that growing up and being gifted brings a budding adolescent. But she learns that she has great inner strength and that yearning to be like others has definite drawbacks. She learns also that parents are not infallible. As much as she wanted her father to save Charles Wallace, he could not. And Meg is surprised to find that she is able to save her brother. Meg is an example of the flawed hero who goes into the world, accomplishes a great deed by thwarting the evil monster in the face of enormous danger, and comes back a changed and more mature individual.

Two of L'Engle's favorite images are the wind and the night sky. The wind weaves its way through the entire time travel series. In *A Wrinkle in Time*, it is associated with the guardian angels. Because of this, some readers see it as a symbol of the Holy Spirit. The luminous sky also occurs as a constant theme in both her fiction and nonfiction. On Uriel the children look at the night sky through a thin atmosphere and see many stars. But, sadly, the sky in *Wrinkle* is also marred by the dark shadow of evil. L'Engle recalls the first instance of being shown the night sky as a small child at her grandmother's home in Florida. She says it was an amazing experience and her first awareness of the size, depth, and excitement of the universe.

Madeleine L'Engle has written in her nonfiction about "the butterfly effect," an idea she borrowed from an astrophysicist that signifies the interrelatedness of everything in the universe. According to chaotic dynamics theory, an event such as a butterfly flapping its wings can begin a chain of events that may cause a large-scale event like a tornado elsewhere in the world. *A Wrinkle in Time* illustrates the responsibility that humans have to care about the universe, since even the smallest actions might be felt by others. Through the journey to save Father and Meg's act of love for her brother, the children's actions reverberate throughout the solar system and join with the forces of good against the powers of evil.

A Wrinkle in Time has been called a science fantasy, a genre that mixes elements from science fiction and fantasy. It has been likened to *Alice in Wonderland* in an essay by Virginia L. Wolf:

> Both Meg and Harriet [in *Harriet the Spy*] are alienated, alone and unhappy.... Both [books are] about a heroine's journeys among characters and through places very much like those found in *Alice in Wonderland* and *Through the Looking Glass*.[11]

Madeleine L'Engle credits her mother with naming the book during a night she had insomnia. Madeleine went into her room with a cup of coffee in the morning and she said, "I think I have a title for your book, and it's right out of the text."[12] L'Engle also says, "If I've ever written a book that says what I feel about God and the universe, this is it. This is my psalm of praise."[13]

Chapter 7

Many Waters

Many Waters, the fourth book in Madeleine L'Engle's Time Quartet, was written in 1986, twenty-four years after *A Wrinkle in Time*. Chronologically it comes between *A Wind in the Door* and *A Swiftly Tilting Planet*. *An Acceptable Time*, her fifth and final science fantasy about Meg and Calvin's daughter, Polly O'Keefe, followed three years later in 1989. *Many Waters* has been challenged by critics for confusing children with a retelling of the story of Noah.

An Accidental Journey

Many Waters stars the adolescent twins, Dennys and Sandy. Their sister, Meg, is commuting to college, and Charles Wallace is about ten years old. On a brittle, wintry day, the boys come in freezing from hockey practice and go searching for cocoa in their parents' lab, ignoring the sign that says, "Experiment in Progress: Keep Out!" Goofing around, they type "Take me someplace warm," then "Someplace warm and sparsely populated" into their dad's computer.[1] Returning to the kitchen, they open the door, feel a blast of heat, and hear a sonic boom. Fearing a fire, they are shocked to find they are no longer in the kitchen, but standing on sand in a burning hot desert.

A small, dark person appears. He is alarmed by the disoriented six-foot-tall twins, who look like giants to him, and thinks he is seeing double. They learn his name is Japheth and that he is dowsing for water with his grandfather's pet mammoth, Higgaion. Hig is the size of a small dog or cat. Surprisingly, they understand Japheth's speech, and they agree to go with him to Grandfather Lamech's tent. The intense heat is too much for the boys. Their skin has become cold and clammy, and Japheth fears they have sun sickness. Hig calls for two silvery grey unicorns, which materialize to carry the twins. Dennys, who has difficulty staying on the unicorn's back, loses consciousness and suddenly vanishes with his unicorn. Sandy holds on until he drops to the ground at Grandfather Lamech's oasis.

Although *Many Waters* is similar to *A Wrinkle in Time* because it begins with a trip through altered time and space, the twins have not deliberately set out on a quest. They are thrust into an adventure as a consequence of their thoughtless actions. Although their siblings have time traveled, the twins are usually minor characters in the stories compared to the more adventurous Meg and Charles Wallace. They are the family realists, who usually reject what they cannot see with their own eyes. However, they have grown up hearing about tesseracts and time travel, so they have little trouble believing that their actions have sent them somewhere into the universe. They just do not know where. Clusters of earthquakes make them wonder if they are on a very young planet. If Charles Wallace had been along, he would have recognized Lamech and Japheth from his bedtime readings of Genesis. In *Many Waters*, L'Engle marries her talent for writing fantasy with her lifelong passion for Bible stories.

Dennys Disappears

When Sandy awakens, he meets Grandfather Lamech and finds that his brother is missing. Japheth agrees to go and look for Dennys. Suddenly a manticore—a creature with a scorpion's tail, lion's body, and a man's head—rushes into the tent, screeching and trying to devour the little mammoth. When grandfather tries to stop him, he sends the old man flying across the tent. Sandy stands up and scares the beast away. Japheth's sister, Yalith, arrives with a lamp for her grandfather. Though tiny like the rest of her people compared to the twins, she is beautiful, and Sandy is instantly attracted to her. Grandfather Lamech causes Adnarel, a golden-winged seraph, to appear. Alarid, another seraph, appears in the form of a pelican to fetch water for Sandy's sunburned body. It is evident that these seraphim are wise and all knowing as well as able to change shape on demand. Adnarel says Sandy must have some knowledge of the "old language," since he is able to talk to grandfather and Japheth.

Many readers have heard of seraphim (the plural of seraph), a type of angel mentioned in the Bible. Most will not be familiar with another type of character L'Engle refers to: nephilim (the plural of nephil). According to legend, nephilim were the offspring of fallen angels. In *Many Waters*, both seraphim and nephilim appear in different forms, looking like animals or human beings.

On her way home, Yalith encounters Eblis, a nephil who says that the life span of human beings is going to be cut short. Yalith is still a child at nearly a hundred years old; her great-grandfather Methuselah lived 969 years, and her father, Noah, is already 600 years old. A lion appears, and transforms into the seraphim Aariel. He warns Eblis to leave Yalith alone, for he knows that Eblis is devious and attracted to the girl.

Dennys awakens in a tent surrounded by several disheveled, angry men. Their sister, Tiglah, has summoned Dennys's unicorn. They think Dennys is some kind of giant and dispose of him on the village garbage dump. Dennys panics and crawls out of the rubbish pit, with no clue where he is. Sobbing and shivering from fever, he tries to summon a unicorn with the help of the family's scraggly mammoth, who has followed him to the dump. When the unicorn materializes, Dennys is too sick to mount properly and throws himself over the unicorn's back.

Dennys and the unicorn reappear in Noah's family tent, which angers Noah. At first Yalith believes he is

Sandy, but then Japheth recognizes Dennys as the twin who is missing. Matred, Noah's wife, calms Noah's anger, pointing out that the boy is extremely ill. Japheth carries Dennys to the women's tent to heal. Sick as he is, Dennys can hear the women talking about the cruelty amongst the people of the land and the falling-out between Noah and his father. Even in his illness, Dennys notices the lovely young Yalith who helps to care for him.

When Sandy feels better, he goes outside with Grandfather Lamech to observe the blackest of skies and the brightest of stars. Grandfather tells him that he is lonely and living in end times. There is a curse upon the ground because of the disobedience of his ancestors. His son, Noah, has grown proud in his prosperity. He is stubborn and will not talk to him because Lamech wishes to remain in his own tent. Lamech tells Sandy that El says his long days are numbered. Sandy wonders who El is, and he is shocked when he hears that Lamech is 777 years old.

Although confused about his location, Sandy feels a sense of discomfort when Lamech mentions a curse. The curse grandfather refers to is found in Chapter 3 of Genesis when Adam and Eve are sent out of the Garden in punishment for eating the forbidden fruit. Noah talks about men's hearts turning to evil. In Chapter 6 of Genesis, God ponders the wickedness of humankind and the decision to wipe them from the earth. The boys, having attended church with their family, are not totally ignorant about the Bible. L'Engle is following the

Madeleine L'Engle receives the Newbery Medal in 1963. Like *A Wrinkle in Time*, *Many Waters* deals with alterations in space and time as well as big philosophical questions.

Biblical story and laying out clues for the twins. Several characters refer to God as El, which means "the Lord" in ancient Hebrew. In her various writings, L'Engle often uses the word "El" for God. She explains that Beth-el, for instance, means the house of God.[2]

L'Engle has been criticized by those who resent her retelling of the Bible story. Not only has she placed the Murry twins into the story, but she has also given Noah four daughters who do not appear in the Bible. Putting aside the important fact that *Many Waters* is fiction, the status of women was limited by law and custom in ancient Israel. Daughters were generally not worth mentioning. L'Engle also does not include the fact that Lamech is recorded to have had two wives. In *Many Waters*, Lamech refers to "Noah's mother" instead of "my wife." Through fiction, L'Engle is speculating about what life might have been like for primitive people in ancient times.

L'Engle is clear about her view of the Old Testament. People have criticized her for not believing that the earth was created in the number of days reported in the first chapters of the Bible. She says that she actually does believe that God created the earth, but not that it necessarily took an exact amount of human time. She comments, "Scripture says a thousand years in our sight is but a moment when it is passed," paraphrasing Psalm 90.[3] In *A Circle of Quiet*, she writes:

> The extraordinary ... thing about Genesis is
> not how unscientific it is but how amazingly

accurate it is. How could the ancient Israelites have known the exact order of a theory of evolution that wasn't to be formulated by scientists for thousands of years? Here is a truth that cuts across barriers of time and space.[4]

The Twins Are Reunited

Noah visits Dennys in the women's tent. Dennys is feeling well enough to ask some questions. Noah tells him that the seraphim are sons of El. He says the nephilim claim to come from El also but are rumored to be the falling stars flung out of heaven. Noah tells Dennys that El says these are end times and that people's hearts have turned to wickedness. Dennys suggests that Noah and

Through fiction, L'Engle is speculating about what life might have been like for primitive people in ancient times.

his father should reconcile. It finally dawns on Dennys that he and Sandy have landed in the pre-flood desert on their own planet. He wracks his brain to remember his Sunday school lessons about Noah and his family. Later, when Dennys goes out with Yalith and Japheth's wife, Oholibamah, he finds that he can hear the stars speak. They tell him not to fear, but to make peace.

Meanwhile, Sandy decides he is well enough to help out in grandfather's garden to repay the kindness he has received. Acting on Dennys's advice, Noah comes to reconcile with his father and introduces himself to Sandy. Sandy, too, now understands that they are in the time of the Bible. He begins to worry about the coming flood, which he discusses with the seraph Adnarel. They talk about time travel and how the boys might return home. Later, Sandy runs into the beautiful Tiglah, who tries to seduce him. Grandfather Lamech warns Sandy about women like Tiglah.

Dennys is finally well enough to make the trip to grandfather's tent. Reunited, the twins discuss the Bible story and what they should do about the flood. What will happen to them? Will all these people be killed? What about the women in Noah's family? It seems silly to them that God once caused a flood because people were evil. They decide to work in the garden and wait to see what happens. The seraphim wonder if the twins were sent to cause peace between Noah and his father.

In *Many Waters*, the twins are separated and left to face their unusual challenges alone. L'Engle gives the twins parallel experiences. They are both instantly attracted to the beautiful Yalith, one sign that they are growing up. Both, comforted by pet mammoths, are under the care of patriarchs who are told by El that humankind is wicked and hard times are near. Both boys have a hand in reconciling Noah and his father. Each boy, upon hearing the name Noah, realizes where they have landed in their journey. Both speak with all-knowing seraphim who understand their predicament and recognize the boys' gifts. Adnarel tells Sandy that he is intelligent, and Alarid tells Dennys he has a gift for languages. As in *A Wrinkle in Time*, L'Engle has given her protagonists guardian angels for protection and wisdom.

L'Engle uses this novel to reveal each twin's individual uniqueness. She hints at this in the first chapter when Sandy realizes that Dennys pays more attention to their parents' science discussions than he does and seems to understand Meg's college textbook. The reader now learns that Dennys daydreams more than Sandy. He is not an initiator but a thinker; Sandy is the doer. Dennys knows more about sanitation and viruses and germs than Sandy. L'Engle has Sandy discussing time travel with the seraph as he calculates how he and his brother might make it back to the twentieth century. Both boys are able to understand the "old language," but only Dennys has the ability to hear the stars.

As mentioned in Chapter 6, Madeleine L'Engle has been consistently praised for her portrayal of bright, educated women in her fiction. *Many Waters* was published in 1986, and her sensitivity to gender is not as surprising as it was when she wrote *A Wrinkle in Time* nearly a quarter century earlier. She has given Noah four daughters, one of whom is the saintly Yalith. Examples of inclusive language appear in the text, such as her use of the word humankind instead of mankind. At one point, the twins are discussing famous people, and Dennys reminds Sandy that Meg would want them to mention Maria Mitchell, the first famous woman astronomer. They agree that their sister would find the times of Noah very chauvinistic. In fact, Sandy and Dennys decide that the story of Noah and the ark must have been written by a man, since Noah's daughters-in-law are not even named in the account.

L'Engle inserts her theological reflections throughout the text. When Sandy tells his brother that he thought it was supposed to be God who wrote the Bible, Dennys says they might have been taught that in Sunday school when they were small children. But now that they are older, he realizes that the Bible was "set down by lots of people over lots of centuries. It's supposed to be the Word of God, not written by God."[5] Once again L'Engle repeats a favorite theme in answer to her critics—that stories do not have to be literal to be true. This is especially relevant to this retelling of the story of Noah, since the author has significantly altered the original story by adding people who have considerable influence on the main characters.

The Coming Flood

Noah has been told by El to build a boat precisely 300 cubits long, 50 cubits wide, and 30 cubits high. (A cubit is an ancient measurement based on the length of the forearm, or about eighteen inches.) On this boat he is to take his three sons and their wives as well as a male and female of each animal species. This is a strange request for people who live in the middle of a desert.

Sandy and Dennys realize that Lamech is dying. Sandy goes to fetch Noah, and on his return, he is abducted by Tiglah's father and brother, working on behalf of the nephilim. They hide him in a tent, planning to ransom him for Noah's vineyards. Tiglah brings the nephil Rofocale, who tells Sandy that he believes the twins have been sent to cause trouble for the nephilim.

When the family's scraggly mammoth comes into the tent, Sandy is reminded that he can call a unicorn to come to his rescue. The unicorn arrives, and his bright shimmer allows Higgaion and Japheth to find Sandy's location. Sandy, the mammoth, and the unicorn fade out, leaving Hig and Japheth to face Tiglah's angry father and brother. Japheth is wounded, but he and Hig escape through the back of the tent.

Sandy decides that he and his brother will help Noah build the ark and then take a quantum leap back home with the assistance of the seraphim. The twins confess to each other that they both love Yalith and are worried what will become of her. When Dennys shares their concerns with Alarid, he says the seraphim are listening for guidance. Although the twins know they cannot change the story, they also realize now that they, themselves, have been changed by all their experiences. Yalith has been told by the stars not to worry. Dennys does not tell Sandy that he, too, has been told by the stars to have patience and wait.

Still plotting against the twins, the nephilim attempt to capture them in the desert but the boys are saved by the seraphim who order the nephilim to leave just as it starts to rain. The seraphim and the twins join in a circle surrounding Yalith and Aariel, who tells her that El has told them to save her as he saved her great grandfather Enoch. She will not have to drown; the seraphim will take her directly to El. Before going, she tells the twins, "Many waters cannot quench love. . . . Neither can the floods drown it."[6] She tells them she loves them. Then, rising into the air in the wings of the seraph, she disappears.

Early the next morning, the twins get dressed in their old clothing and summon the unicorns. The seraphim Admael and Adnarel go to the twentieth century and call for the unicorns. Alarid and Aariel stay in the desert to send the unicorns with the boys to their home. The seraphim decide that El did not send the twins, but neither did El prevent them from coming. Adnarel thinks that the twins were part of a pattern that is not set, but ever changing. "But it will be worked out in beauty in the end. Admael affirmed."[7]

Madeleine L'Engle's recreation of the story of the flood interweaves the biblical account with familiar characters from the Murry family. As in much of her other fiction, this is a "coming-of-age" novel for the protagonists. The twins prove to be more interesting than previously portrayed in other books. Their strange experience, just as they are growing into manhood, forces them to take responsibility and make hard moral decisions. As Meg did during *A Wrinkle in Time*, in *Many Waters* the twins mature into responsible young people. They learn to have patience and faith in what they cannot understand.

106

L'Engle again emphasizes the importance of family. The boys are disturbed by the rift between Noah and his father. Sandy tells Lamech that perhaps Noah is stubborn because his father is stubborn, and he suggests that Lamech go see Noah. Dennys pushes Noah to help his father. They are praised for causing the reunion between father and son, and for helping Noah to be a better person. The Bible says that God chose Noah's family to repopulate the earth because he was a good man. *In Many Waters*, El asks Noah to build the ark after he makes up with his father. The seraphim believe that the boys were responsible for bringing out Noah's goodness. Has the author given the boys a starring role in God's choice of Noah? Or is L'Engle showing the reader that Noah's goodness could have been the result of loving acts shown toward him—reminding the reader that every action ripples into the universe and has consequences?

The twins fit into Noah's family because of their own experiences. They tend Enoch's garden because they are used to pulling their weight in their own home. They are drawn to the small mammoths just as they are drawn to the family dog. As odd as their experience might be, much of it feels like home to them. L'Engle once again tells readers that family remains important in the face of difficult times. Families take care of the living and the dying, they worry about each other, they support one another, and they come to the rescue of those in need.

L'Engle takes the legendary seraphim and nephilim and places them in tension with one another. She presents the nephilim not as horrible monsters, but as self-indulgent. They are evil because they have chosen to turn away from El, which is the ultimate sin. The twins are confronted with several choices themselves. Sandy rebuffs Tiglah and resists her wiles on several occasions. While he is in captivity, he declares that violence is never an option to solve problems. Both boys decide to put their trust in El to save Yalith just as they avoid making their love for her an issue between them. They relinquish control over their own destiny and trust that they will, themselves, be saved from the flood. These are mature choices for adults, let alone adolescents, and are examples of their growing faith and maturity.

L'Engle has Sandy and Dennys discuss entropy, which is a subject they have read about in school. Entropy is the process of degradation, or running down, of matter and energy. Sandy does not like the idea that the universe might be winding down. He is disturbed that Noah's society will be wiped out by El. Dennys counters that natural disasters always affect innocent victims. He questions the theory of entropy. He believes that there is no such thing as an unbreakable scientific rule: "because sooner or later, they all seem to get broken ... or to change."[8] Dennys believes that the universe is still being born and the flood is part of the birth process. He says, "There have been many times of last days,... and they mark not only endings

108

but beginnings."[9] Sandy wonders if there is a pattern to it all or if it is chaos. In this dialogue between the boys, L'Engle points to the ebb and flow of natural events and the opportunity for rebirth in the midst of chaos. Further, she shows a belief in an underlying purpose or meaning behind the events in the universe.

Some familiar themes from other novels also appear in *Many Waters*. Sandy and Dennys join L'Engle's other protagonists by being awed by the night sky. Yalith tells Dennys that the starlight is healing, and he is amazed at the stars in the clear atmosphere. When Sandy and Lamech sit under the night sky, Sandy is awed by the radiance of the stars and the blackness of the firmament. Dennys understands the song of the stars telling him not to be afraid and to wait and have patience. He also listens to the song of the wind, a theme that blows through the entire Time series.

L'Engle has been praised for her retelling of Bible stories. In *Many Waters*, the reader has a sense of what people might have experienced in Noah's time as seen through the eyes of the twins. The name *Many Waters* comes from Yalith's message to the boys as she leaves the world. "Many waters cannot quench love... Neither can the floods drown it." These words are from Chapter 8, Verse 7, in the Songs of Songs. Written as a series of love poems, they are often interpreted as a picture of the loving relationship between God and God's people. In using these words, L'Engle once again suggests to her readers that love is the most powerful force in the universe.

Chapter 8

Challenges to L'Engle's Work

Formulating statistics on attempts to ban books is far from an exact science. In fact, it is nearly impossible to be accurate. The American Library Association (ALA) compiles a database from incidents reported in newspapers across the country and from individuals who contact the ALA to report local challenges to books. When an individual reports a challenge, the ALA enters into its databases only the title of the book, the type of institution receiving the challenge, and the state in which the challenge occurred in order to respect confidentiality of the reporter. A bimonthly newsletter contains the reports that are then compiled in the Banned Books Resource Guide every year. The ALA has a form on its Web site for people to use if they wish to make a report. However, the organization says its research shows that more than 75 percent of challenges are unreported.[1]

Other agencies compile reports as well. The National Council of Teachers of English (NCTE) gathers challenge information through their Web site. Their periodic censorship reports contain information about challenged books and other news on censorship attempts across the nation. The National Coalition Against Censorship is another organization that provides a Web site link to report concerns. Between 1985 and 1996, People for the American Way (PAW) produced annual reports documenting attempts to remove books and other materials from schools and libraries. The information from these various sources does not always overlap.

Gathering Statistics

In 2006, the ALA Office for Intellectual Freedom received reports of a total of 546 challenges filed with libraries in the United States requesting that materials be removed because of the content itself or the age-appropriateness of the content.[2] The ALA categorized

Censorship Challenges by Categories, 1990–2000

1,607 books challenged for "sexually explicit" material

1,427 challenged for "offensive language"

1,256 challenged for material "unsuited to age group"

842 challenged for having an "occult theme or promoting the occult or Satanism"

737 challenged for material considered "violent"

515 challenged for having a homosexual theme or "promoting homosexuality"

419 challenged for material "promoting a religious viewpoint"

317 challenged for containing "nudity"

267 challenged for containing "racism"

224 challenged for pertaining to "sex education"

202 challenged for containing material considered "anti-family"

the reasons for each complaint as well as listing the challenge attempts. Challenged materials can fall into more than one category. Of the top ten most challenged books in 2005, "sexual content" and "offensive language" were the two most prevalent concerns. From 1990 to 2000, there were 6,364 challenges reported. Again, "sexually explicit" material and "offensive language," closely followed by "unsuited to age group," were the highest offenders.[3]

The Office of Intellectual Freedom at the American Library Association also publishes a list of the most frequently challenged authors. An author might appear on this list, but not on the most challenged books list. For instance, Judy Blume might have several books with only one challenge each. They would not appear on the list of most challenged books, but because she is prolific and controversial in the eyes of some readers, she has consistently appeared on the most challenged author list.

Each year since 1982, a coalition of organizations made up of the American Booksellers Foundation for Free Expression, the American Library Association, the Association of American Publishers, the American Society of Journalists and Authors, and the National Association of College Stores cosponsor "Banned Books Week: Celebrating the Freedom to Read" during the month of September. Booksellers, schools, and libraries interested in participating in the event are sent kits of materials that help to raise awareness of censorship and promote education about the freedom to read. There has been some criticism of the title "Banned Books Week," since the majority of books challenged do not end up being removed from library shelves. The ALA suggests that the title is appropriate because "a challenge is an attempt to ban or restrict materials, based upon the objection of a person or group. A successful challenge would result in materials being banned or restricted."[4]

Dan Cherubin, in his article "Creating the Acceptable Taboo," raises concerns about Banned Books Week and suggests that books, even when removed from the library shelves, are far from being banned, because they are widely available to consumers. Further, he says, "this is a remarkably keen marketing scheme. [It] promotes reading to children, not by extolling the virtue of reading [the book], but by telling [children] that adults do not want them to read it."[5] Tom Minnery, vice president of public policy for Focus on the Family, a conservative organization, writes:

> Nothing is banned, but every year this organization [ALA] attempts to intimidate and silence any parent, teacher or librarian who expresses concern about the age-appropriateness of sexually explicit or violent material for schoolchildren.[6]

People usually challenge books with the best intentions. They wish to protect others, especially their children, from reading about topics they think are harmful or difficult to understand. Often challenges are made to protect children from reading about ideas that are contrary to a parent's belief system. Many people believe that information should be banned that would compromise their vision of the highest ideals of society.

As previously mentioned, in America, freedom of speech has been supported over and over by the Constitution and upheld by the courts. Historically, book banning was under the controlling efforts of the

Celebrate the right to read.

Banned Books Week
September 23-30, 2006

This poster from the American Library Association advertises Banned Books Week.

state, the church, or other authorities. As ideals of individual freedom grew, and these traditional authority groups were challenged over the years, the focus shifted. People began to have differing ideas about who should have the power to act as a watchdog for our society—which is protected by a Constitution that assures freedom of speech and expression to all its citizens. No one would question the right of a parent to guide his or her own children's reading material. However, some would say that the attempt to remove a book from a library is an attempt to impose those views on other parents' children by restricting what they are able to read and denying their First Amendment rights. Others would disagree because they believe that some books pose a danger to the community. They believe that citizens ought to have a say in what books are bought for tax-supported institutions such as public schools as well as a voice in upholding high standards for the community. Furthermore, they do not want their children stigmatized or separated from their classmates by having to read alternative assignments.

Challenges to *A Wrinkle in Time*

According to available statistics, there have been over thirty reported attempts to remove *A Wrinkle in Time* from library shelves since 1990. In 1985, there was attempt to remove the book from an elementary school media center in Polk City, Florida. A student's parent filed the complaint because she felt the story promoted witchcraft, crystal balls, and demons. The book was retained. In 1990, a challenge arose in the schools in Anniston, Alabama. One student's father claimed that the novel dealt with New Age religion and sent a mixed signal to children about good and evil, since witches are among the fantasy creatures that help the young characters. He was also concerned that L'Engle had listed the name of Jesus Christ together with the names of great artists, philosophers, scientists, and religious

115

leaders when referring to defenders of the earth against evil as if they were the same importance:

> *"Who have our fighters been?"*
> *Calvin asked....*
>
> *"Jesus!" Charles Wallace said. "Why of course, Jesus!"*
>
> *"Of course," Mrs Whatsit said. "Go on, Charles, love. There were others. All your great artists. They've been lights for us to see by."*
>
> *"Leonardo da Vinci?" Calvin suggested tentatively. "And Michaelangelo?"*
>
> *"And Shakespeare," Charles Wallace called out, "and Bach! And Pasteur and Madame Curie and Einstein!"*[7]

School officials told the student's father that many, including his son, had purchased the book on their own. He responded that he had withdrawn his son from the school because the book had been read to him and he had been allowed to purchase it. The request to ban the book was denied by the board of education.[8]

In 1989, a father in Hood River, Oregon, did not want his fifth-grade son assigned *A Wrinkle in Time* because the theme of the book was "demonistic magical power" based on his reading of two chapters and the book's cover. The review committee corresponded with the author and recommended that the school board retain the book. In a letter to district officials, Madeleine L'Engle wrote:

> Alas, I suspect the parent who sees witchcraft and sorcery in *A Wrinkle in Time* calls her/himself a "Christian." Thus far, it has been only "Christians" who have misunderstood and attacked this book. We find what we look for, we human beings, and if a parent is looking for witchcraft and sorcery, that parent is going to find it whether it's there or not. And of course, *A Wrinkle in Time* is about neither.... I see the book as my affirmation of a God of love.[9]

Later, school officials found that the book had disappeared from three district libraries and the local public library.

In 1990, a parent and a pastor in El Paso, Texas, objected to the use of the book in the sixth grade. They claimed that it represented New Age religion and would produce "confusion, anti-family units, and anti-Christian values." They felt the book made "no valuable contribution" and "the only possible point ... is to ... confuse the children who are Christians." The school district's review committee disagreed. It said that the book's overall theme is love for one's family. They also indicated that the idea of New Age religion had not even been conceived when the book was written.[10] In 1991, parents in Anchorage, Alaska, wished to remove the book, along with *The Witch of Blackbird Pond* by

Elizabeth Speare, for alleged Satanism and "dead people speaking through [a] medium." Again, the books were retained.[11]

Three other incidents were compiled by PAW in 1991. In Rialto, California, a group of sixth-grade parents disagreed with the inclusion of *A Wrinkle in Time* in the curriculum because, they said, it was a frightening book that encouraged students to believe in fantasy. Again, a review committee noted the book's universal values and literary merit.[12] In Snellville, Georgia, parents claimed that the book exposed fifth graders to mysticism, Far Eastern religious practices, and New Age beliefs.[13] In Waterloo, Iowa, parents alleged "cult implications," "sadism," "Satanic suggestions," and "indoctrination in the Occult." They also complained that *L'Engle* listed Jesus in a group of great artists but did not distinguish him as being any different or acknowledge that he was the son of God. A review committee voted to retain the book in both the classroom and the media center.[14]

Another example of the power challenges can have took place in Needles, California, in 1993. Parents objected to the use of *A Wrinkle in Time* in a fifth-grade classroom because they felt it had satanic content. After receiving the complaint, the principal and four teachers removed the book from the reading list, even though the parents had only requested that their children be given an alternative assignment.[15] In 1996, the book was challenged in Newton, North Carolina. A parent wanted it removed from the school library because, he

118

said, it undermined religious beliefs. Evidently his child had complained to him about the book when it was assigned to her academically gifted class. The father voiced his objection to school officials, who offered an alternative assignment. But he wanted it pulled from all the school libraries. He told the school board that it made references to the occult, witchcraft, and mysticism. The board voted unanimously to keep the book, saying he had the right to choose for his daughter but not the other children.[16]

In Livingston County, New York, a mother objected to the book along with all books dealing with the occult and Halloween. She wanted them removed from the elementary school library. The principal did not comply, since no formal complaint had been filed and the objection was based on the cover illustration and synopsis of the book. It was suggested that the parent come back after reading the novel, but she rejected the suggestion and claimed that "the devil was making the principal suggest this."[17]

In April 1996, the Antioch, California, school board voted 4 to 1 to refuse a parent's request for her daughter to read an alternative assignment to *A Wrinkle in Time*. She claimed the book violated her religious beliefs because of its references to magic and mind reading. The school superintendent indicated that the district could not allow parents to set their own academic standards.[18] This was an unusual decision, since most schools use alternative assignments as one way to serve parents when they disagree with the curriculum. It is not unusual for students to be routinely excused from various activities on religious grounds.

In 1999, the NCTE publication "From the Front Line," reported that a parent wished to remove *A Wrinkle in Time* from an Oklahoma high school because of "religious reasons."[19]

Challenges to the novel have declined in the last few years; however, Nanette Perez, project coordinator for the American Library Association Office of Intellectual Freedom, reports that there have been five challenges citing religious viewpoints or the occult/Satanism since 2000 in Texas, Illinois, Missouri, and Georgia.[20]

Ninety-five percent of people who challenge *A Wrinkle in Time* use the terms "occult," "Satanism," "anti-Christian," or "New Age" in their reasons for why they think the book is dangerous for children to read. It might be presumed that L'Engle's use of magic in the novel is the impetus for these concerns. Certainly the reference to New Age must be based on characters such as Charles Wallace who have extrasensory powers and the fact that the challengers believe the three Mrs are witches and the Happy Medium a sorceress. Over and over, challengers mention a concern that the novel will undermine children's religious beliefs. One category mentioned that seems confusing is "sexually explicit content." The mild flirtation between Calvin and Meg could hardly fit that description.

120

Other Challenges

In 1991, the Office of Intellectual Freedom of the American Library Association ranked Madeleine L'Engle number nine in its list of the top ten banned authors. Although *A Wrinkle in Time* is responsible for most of the statistics, other novels have made the list.

The second book of L'Engle's that has been repeatedly challenged in schools is *Many Waters*. The concern about the novel *Many Waters* is straightforward. L'Engle's critics do not agree with her changing any part of the Bible for fear she will confuse her young readers and alter their perception of the biblical story. It was challenged at a Hubbard, Ohio, library in 1991 because it was accused of altering the story of Noah's Ark, which according to the challenger made it secular and confused children.[21] The ALA reported that it was also challenged in Maine and Kansas and a fourth unspecified state.

Two other young adult books by L'Engle have met with objections, according to PAW and the American Library Association: *And Both Were Young* and *A House Like a Lotus*. The second book, L'Engle's novel about Polly O'Keefe, was challenged in the state of Texas in 2004 by a public library patron who declared it unsuitable for the young adult age group. They objected because Polly's friends were homosexual and the book included the word "champagne."[22]

It is surprising to many that *A Wrinkle in Time* and *Many Waters* have been challenged when two other books in the Time series—*A Swiftly Tilting Planet* and *A*

Wind in the Door, which have very similar content— have not. Madeleine L'Engle claims that *A Wind in the Door* was also cited once in a midwestern newspaper article listing ten books to be removed from library shelves because of their pornographic content. This totally baffled her, because she could find nothing that she had written that was remotely pornographic.

Sometimes people lodging complaints against books have been accompanied by representatives of organizations such as Citizens for Excellence in Education, a conservative Christian group that helps individuals address local public school issues. More often, challengers cited information from books from organizations such as James Dobson's Focus on the Family and the Eagle Forum, two conservative organizations that work to preserve traditional values in the United States.

Another Point of View

In Carole Chase's book *Madeleine L'Engle, Suncatcher*, L'Engle's friend Luci Shaw writes,

> Madeleine is an explorer and a boundary-breaker. She has also been called a "universe disturber," but such a term never implies destruction or malicious disruption. If she shakes up her readers with radical ideas, it is because she is convinced of their truth and necessity, and that, as one who catches light from God, it is her responsibility to beam it into our imaginations.[23]

122

L'Engle is a fiction writer. Her imagination ranges from one planet to the next. Her characters fly through space and have guardian angels. She is captivated by the marvels of science and the universe. She wonders aloud what it might have been like in the time of Noah or what would happen if Noah had daughters as well as sons. Her wondering has taken millions of children into different worlds, and she differs from her critics by believing that it is healthy and exciting to wonder. She states that according to her critics, "anything that mentions ghosts, witches, spirits, has to go ... [but] if that is taken literally, the Bible will have to be added to the pyre: because of Saul and the witch of Endor and Samuel's ghost."[24] Her critics have accused her of putting Jesus on par with Einstein and Buddha. She disagrees and feels that people who read her books are putting their own interpretation to her words.

Although L'Engle has often addressed the subject of censorship in her writing and her talks throughout the country, she has not given undue attention to individuals who write against her or attempt to ban her books. She indicates that most protests that come directly to her are from people, not students, who attend her university lectures and "who've decided ahead of time what they think I think."[25] Speaking about the problem of people interfering with public and school library book decisions in her Library of Congress address, she says, "I have enormous respect and admiration and love for the librarians who are rising up to protest this, because they are putting their very jobs on

123

the line."[26] In her book *Penguins and Golden Calves*, she writes about the incident when she heard her critics on the air. She refused to name the speaker or the book she coauthored against L'Engle "because I do not want to give that kind of hate any publicity."[27] Later she commented on the book that she said was full of lies and distortions. "I don't intend to 'do' anything about it…. I don't want to meet hate with hate or even defensiveness."[28]

The challenges to Madeleine L'Engle's works have waned somewhat in the past few years. Perhaps it is because most censorship attempts have not been successful. It might be because the new breed of children's authors have become more realistic and bold in their fiction than she. It may be because there is not a consensus among Christian fundamentalists about her work. L'Engle has been open in sharing her beliefs with readers of her many nonfiction books as well as her overtly religious works. She has been the guest speaker at churches and organizations ranging across the spectrum from those who are more fundamental and literal in their Christian faith to those who have a great tolerance for diversity. She has a strong following in all sides of the religious spectrum, including people who claim no religious affiliation at all. As a prolific and respected American author, her religious beliefs are secondary to her amazing talent for telling a story.

Chapter 9

The Legacy of Madeleine L'Engle

Those who knew Madeleine L'Engle described her as a tall and elegant woman who wore unconventional, long flowing skirts and tunics and dangling earrings. Her gray hair was cut short and she had a no-nonsense attitude. When she spoke, she was terse and to the point.[1] All her life she loved to read. She credited that lifelong love of books from when she was three or four and her family took her to the Norfolk, Connecticut, library reading room. As an adult, she enjoyed reading work by good mystery writers. She appreciated British mysteries because, she said, they often have an honorable point of view—the protagonists are usually decent characters who want to learn why people do awful things. She also enjoyed reading light fiction and scientific articles.

The Teacher

Madeleine L'Engle had the heart of a good teacher. She told her students that she was a very stubborn woman. However, she pointed out that a person's faults might also be virtues in the right circumstances. L'Engle felt that her stubbornness often made her very difficult to live with. But it was also the trait that kept her going during all the years she was receiving rejection slips for her books. She simply refused to give up on being a writer.

Madeleine L'Engle in her office at the Cathedral of St. John the Divine in New York City. L'Engle incorporated many aspects of religion and spirituality in her books for children as well as adults.

Because of her active imagination and lifelong love of words, she wrote daily and kept journals throughout her life. Thomas Howard described her as a poet as opposed to a philosopher, who is logical, rational, favoring words over ideas or substance. Howard says that L'Engle reached for the "vocabulary of myth, image and sacrament as she [grappled] with what matters about the universe." He indicated that the vocabulary of the two parties differs. "The philosophers sometimes suspect that the poets believe in elves."[2] Similarly, L'Engle's visionary spirit is captured by artist and poet Brian Andreas when he writes about a conversation between a philosopher and a poet: "She kept asking if the stories were true. I kept asking her if it mattered. We finally gave up. She was looking for a place to stand and I wanted a place to fly."[3]

This preference in worldview and the way L'Engle thought is at the heart of the matter. It was the difference between her and her critics. She was drawn to mystery and embraced the mysteries of life. She did not thrive on pat answers and doctrine. Her preference could be seen in her choice of denomination, the Episcopal Church, where the mystery of the Eucharist, or communion, is at the heart of the service of worship. A respect for poetic language can be seen in its use of the Book of Common Prayer. And it is a denomination that embraces a number of points of view without an emphasis on strict doctrine. L'Engle and her critics both stood firmly within the Christian religion while holding very different interpretations of faith.

The Artist

Donald R. Hettinga comments that is it not surprising that Madeleine L'Engle's fantasy fiction is open to theological questions from her critics because she herself wrote that "her fantasy is her theology."[4] She believed her gift came from God. However, her theology cannot be found in the religious content of her novels, but in a deeper understanding of the underlying events and actions of her characters. L'Engle invites readers to dig deep, to perceive the themes of the stories she creates. Her characters reflect true life as they show doubt and confusion, fear and hope, failure and triumph in their journeys. L'Engle's novels are fiction, and they are not intended to be read as actual fact. That does not keep them from pointing to important truths about the nature of the universe, about humans, and about her belief in the tenets of her Christian faith. L'Engle indicated that she did not write for a Christian audience. She believed that Christianity is not a fearful religion, but an affirmative one that acknowledges that every person matters. She wrote:

> "If we fall into [a] trap of assuming that other people are not Christians because they do not belong to our own particular brand of Christianity, no wonder we become incapable of understanding the works of art produced by so-called non-Christians, whether they be atheists, Jews, Buddhists, or anything else outside a frame of reference we have made into a closed rather than an open door."[5]

Misunderstanding often exists between artists and observers, writers and readers, because creators of great art use elements that may offend for the purpose of revealing the truth about a subject. Novice viewers may be "put off" by a piece of modern art until an education gives them a perspective and understanding of the artist's intent and they gain respect and appreciation for the work. An understanding of L'Engle's perspective on faith helps the reader to understand why she wrote as she did. L'Engle's intention was not to reiterate doctrine to fellow Christians. "If I understand the Gospel, it tells us that we are to spread the Good News to all four corners of the world.... If my stories are incomprehensible to Jews or Muslims, or Taoists, then I have failed as a Christian writer."[6] She believed that God's grace can only shine through characters in her books if they are imperfect just as humans are imperfect. "Fiction must tell the truth. Fiction written by Christians ought to tell the truth about the brokenness in the world, and it ought to give us a glimpse of what it will mean for the lion to lie down with the lamb."[7]

The Believer

As an adult, L'Engle commented that she was a happy agnostic. When she was a college student, she read philosophy and opted for the world of the intellect and mind alone. She called herself an unhappy agnostic because she was always seeking answers that were not available. To L'Engle, the word *agnostic* simply meant that she could not know everything with her finite mind. She said that intellect is a poor instrument for comprehending all the truths of the universe. "It does not mean that I do not believe, it is an acceptance that I am created, that I am asked to bear the light, knowing that this is the most wonderful of all vocations."[8]

Fellow author Walter Wangerin, Jr., said of L'Engle: "The public personality and the private person are the same. This woman wears no mask to please a paying multitude. The temperate, insightful, affectionate, galactic, and homely L'Engle whom we meet in the book—that is L'Engle." He noted that the private person who was literate, devout, and faithful was the same as the quick-witted and personable woman at the podium.[9]

The Friend

Luci Shaw was a close friend of L'Engle's for nearly forty years. As her editor, publisher, writing partner, fellow lecturer, and traveling companion, she shared many of life's significant experiences, such as the year when both lost their husbands to cancer. Shaw's deep affection and appreciation for her friend show in the writing projects they shared over the years. Both of them mentioned the time when they were going over a manuscript of L'Engle's, when Shaw commented on a passage. "Madeleine, you can't say that!" she exclaimed, not wanting readers to be offended or so angry they stopped reading. After a heated discussion with her friend, Shaw admitted: "I realized that what Madeleine had to say was meant to make people think, to move them out of their ruts, and that what she had to say was important, even vital."[10]

L'Engle was a gracious and forgiving woman with a great sense of humor. When verbally attacked, she was determined to emulate her hero, Mahatma Gandhi, responding graciously and not trying to "get even." Generous to struggling artists, she was an active member of the Chrysostom Society, a group of Christian writers that encourages and supports younger artists.

Shaw and L'Engle took several vacations together. As they drove or traveled, they would make up sonnets or nonsense poems, alternating in their invention of the lines. L'Engle always carried along her two journals. In one she noted ideas and events she wanted to

Friends for decades, Madeleine L'Engle and Luci Shaw have shared many of life's experiences, including writing projects.

remember. The other was a very private journal, not shared with others. She also brought her laptop computer on trips for work on ongoing novels or poems. Often while driving, L'Engle would become preoccupied, and Shaw would realize that she was writing in her head, eager to stop for the night and work on her computer. Their shared book, *Friends for the Journey*, is a testament to the long and cherished relationship between these two writers and poets.

The Timeless L'Engle

At the time of her death in September 2007, Madeleine L'Engle was less than three months away from her eighty-ninth birthday. She had not been well in recent years. In 2002, she suffered a stroke, and her strength continued to decline. In ill health, she returned to live out her days at her beloved Crosswicks, where she was close to her eldest daughter, Josephine, and other dear friends.

Her books are still in demand and selling strongly. The Time Quartet was reprinted by Farrar, Strauss and Giroux in 2003. Two compilations of her poems and writings have been issued—*Madeleine L'Engle Herself: Reflections on a Writing Life* in 2001 and *The Ordering of Love: The New and Collected Poems of Madeleine L'Engle* in 2005. The reissue of the Time Quintet in 2007 and *The Joys of Love* in 2008 are a testimony to her enormous talent. The works have not faded with time, but have remained alive and timeless. Madeleine L'Engle will always be known as one of the great storytellers of the twentieth century.

Discussion Questions

1. Do you think there should be any reasons for censorship within a democratic society?

2. Do you think that children should have the freedom to read what they wish or to express their opinions, even if those opinions are unpopular or offend their parents or other adults?

3. Do you think there should ever be a time when one parent has a right to decide what other parents' children should read or not read?

4. Do you think that authors writing for young people today go too far with realism?

5. Should all books with materials that might be potentially offensive to any particular group be banned from school libraries and classrooms?

6. How can society honor diversity while respecting each group's particular interests?

7. Do you think it is punitive for students to have alternative assignments when they (or their parents) disagree with the material the class is reading?

8. If you have read any of Madeleine L'Engle's books, do you believe they promote New Age principles or witchcraft?

9. Do you think L'Engle's works should be used in schools? Why or why not?

Timeline

399 B.C.E.—Socrates is put to death for speaking too freely with his students.

1450 C.E.—Gutenberg invents the printing press and publishes the Gutenberg Bible.

1536—William Tyndale is executed for translating and publishing the Bible in English.

1559—Pope Paul IV issues the Index of Forbidden Books, which influenced Roman Catholics in some form until 1948.

1873—Comstock Law is passed in the United States, granting the Post Office authority to confiscate books thought to be "lewd, indecent, filthy or obscene."

1918—Madeleine L'Engle Camp is born on November 29 in New York City.

1929—L'Engle's family moves to Switzerland, where she attends boarding school.

1933—Nazis burn more than 20,000 books in Germany.

1933—L'Engle's family moves back to America.

1935—Penguin issues its first paperback, creating a mass market for books.

1945—L'Engle's first novel, *The Small Rain*, is published.

1946—Madeleine L'Engle marries Hugh Franklin on January 26.

1954—Senator Joseph McCarthy holds hearings to purge the country of Communist sympathizers.

1961—Mel and Norma Gabler begin their textbook challenges.

1962—*A Wrinkle in Time* is published after more than 20 rejections.

1963—L'Engle is awarded the Newbery Medal for *A Wrinkle in Time.*

1969—The Supreme Court upholds students' rights to express their political and social views in *Tinker v. Des Moines Independent School District.*

1975—In *Island Trees v. Pico,* the Supreme Court says school boards do not have the right to remove books from school libraries because they dislike the ideas they contain.

1975—L'Engle is invited to archive her collection at Wheaton College in Illinois.

1983—L'Engle gives the lecture "Dare to Be Creative!" at the Library of Congress.

1991—L'Engle ranks ninth on the American Library Association list of the top ten banned authors.

2004—L'Engle receives the National Humanities Medal from President George W. Bush.

2006—The American Library Association receives 546 challenges to libraries in the United States.

2007—Madeleine L'Engle dies on September 6.

Chapter Notes

Chapter 1.
Meet Madeleine L'Engle

1. Claris Van Kuiken, *Battle to Destroy Truth* (Manassas, Va.: REF Publishing, 1996), p. 74.

2. Brenda Scott and Samantha Smith, *Trojan Horse: How the New Age Movement Infiltrates the Church* (Lafayette, La.: Huntington House, 1993), p. 29.

3. Van Kuiken, p. 26.

4. "The 100 Most Frequently Challenged Books of 1990–2000," American Library Association, n.d., <http://www.ala.org/ala/oif/bannedbooksweek/bbwlinks/100mostfrequently.htm> (May 24, 2006).

5. Ibid.

6. Madeleine L'Engle, *Penguins and Golden Calves: Icons and Idols* (Wheaton, Ill.: Harold Shaw Publishers, 1996), p. 81.

7. Scott and Smith, p. vii.

8. Carole F. Chase, *Madeleine L'Engle, Suncatcher* (San Diego: Lurimedia, 1995), p. 32.

9. Cathleen Rountree, *On Women Turning 70: Honoring the Voices of Wisdom* (San Francisco: Jossey-Bass Publishers, 1999), p. 103.

10. L'Engle, *Penguins and Golden Calves: Icons and Idols*, p. 83.

11. Madeleine L'Engle, *The Rock That Is Higher: Story As Truth* (Wheaton, Ill.: Harold Shaw Publishers, 1993), p. 184.

12. Maria Ruiz Scaperlanda, "Madeleine L'Engle: An Epic in Time," *St. Anthony Messenger*, June 2000,<http://www.americancatholic.org/Messenger/June2000/feature1.asp> (August 29, 2006).

13. Dee Dee Risher, "Listening to the Story: A Conversation with Madeleine L'Engle," *The Other Side Online*, March-April 1998, Vol. 34, No. 2, <http://www.theotherside.org/archive/mar-apr98/lengle.html> (March 21, 2006).

14. Betsy Hearne, "A Mind in Motion," *School Library Journal*, Vol. 44, No. 6, June 1998, pp. 28–33, <http://proquest.umi.com/pqdweb?did=30133305&Fmt=4&clientld=22133&RQT=309&VName=PQD> (January 25, 2006).

15. Van Kuiken.

16. Madeleine L'Engle, "Dare to Be Creative!" a lecture presented at the Library of Congress, November 16, 1983 (Washington, D.C.: Library of Congress, 1984), p. 21.

Chapter 2.
Censorship and Society

1. Ann Lyon Haight, *Banned Books: Informal Notes on Some Books Banned for Various Reasons at Various Times and in Various Places* (New York: R. R. Bowker Company, 1970), p. 3.

2. Nicholas J. Karolides, Margaret Bald, and Dawn B. Sova, *100 Banned Books: Censorship Histories of World Literature* (New York: Checkmark Books, 1999), p. 169.

3. Mette Newth, "The Long History of Censorship," *Beacon for Freedom of Expression*, July 2001, <http://www.beaconforfreedom.org/about_project/history.html> (May 31, 2006).

4. Ibid.

5. Richard Lovelace, "To Althea, from Prison," *Poet's Corner*, n.d., <http://www.theotherpages.org/poems/lovela01.html> (May 3, 2007).

6. Golam M. Sarowar, "134 Journalists Imprisoned, of them 49 Internet Journalists," *iTalknews: Citizen Journalism*, December 14, 2006, <http://www.italknews.com/view_story.php?sid=10610> (March 1, 2007).

7. "In Iraq, Journalist Deaths Spike to Record in 2006," *CPJ Special Report 2006*, December 20, 2006, <http://cpj.org/Briefings/2006/killed_06/killed_06.html> (March 1, 2007).

8. "Fact Sheet on Sex and Censorship," *The Free Expression Policy Project*, n.d., <http://www.fepproject.org/factsheets/sexandcensorship.html> (May 31, 2006).

9. Paul S. Boyer, *Purity in Print: Book Censorship in America* (New York: Scribners and Sons, 1968), p. 14.

10. "Fact Sheet on Sex and Censorship."

11. Madeleine L'Engle, "Dare to Be Creative!" a lecture presented at the Library of Congress, November 16, 1983 (Washington, D.C.: Library of Congress, 1984), p. 17.

12. Boyer, p. 10.

13. Ibid., p. 54.

14. Herbert N. Foerstel, *Banned in the U.S.A.: A Reference Guide to Book Censorship in Schools and Public Libraries* (Westport, Conn.: Greenwood Press, 2002), p. xix.

Chapter 3.
Censorship in Schools and Libraries

1. Mary E. Brown, "A Brief History of Children's Literature," *Literature For Children*, Southern Connecticut State University, n.d., <http://www.southernct.edu/%7Ebrownm/300hlit.html> (May 31, 2006).

2. Cynthia Crossen, "'Abstain From Evil' Was Once a Lesson in Pupils' Textbooks," *The Wall Street Journal*, Monday, August 28, 2006, p. B1.

3. Colleen Corkery and Edith Batalis, "A Century of Education," *Atlanta Parent*, n.d., <http://www.atlanta parent.com/06-01%20January%202006/jan2006-art2.html> (February 3, 2006).

4. Nicholas J. Karolides, Lee Burress, and John M. Kean, eds., *Censored Books: Critical Viewpoints* (Lanham, Md.: The Scarecrow Press, Inc., 2001), p. xix.

5. William Noble, *Bookbanning in America: Who Bans Books—and Why* (Middlebury, Vt.: Paul S. Eriksson Publisher, 1990), p. 182.

6. Lee Burress, *The Battle of the Books: Literary Censorship in Public Schools: 1950–1985* (Metuchen, N.J.: Scarecrow Press, 1989), p. 98.

7. Diane Ravitch, *The Language Police* (New York: Vintage Books, 2004), p. 46.

8. Noble, p. 216.

9. Ravitch, p. 113.

10. "The Language Police/TextbookPC," *Think Tank with Ben Wattenberg*, June 13, 2003, <http://www.pbs.org/thinktank/transcript1116.html> (June 19, 2006).

11. Karolides, Burress, and Kean, p. xvii.

12. Ravitch, p. 113.

13. Madeleine L'Engle, *Penguins and Golden Calves: Icons and Idols* (Wheaton, Ill.: Harold Shaw Publishers, 1996), p. 68.

14. Ravitch, p. 113.

15. Herbert N. Foerstel, *Banned in the U.S.A.: A Reference Guide to Book Censorship in Schools and Public Libraries* (Westport, Conn.: Greenwood Press, 2002), p. 66.

16. "Schools and Censorship," *People for the American Way: Public Education*, n.d., <http://www.pfaw.org/pfaw/general/default.aspx?oid=11652> (February 18, 2006).

17. Dave Jenkinson and Pat Bolger, "Censorship," *A Reviewing Journal of Canadian Materials for Young People*, Vol. 18, No. 3, May 1990, <http://www.umanitoba.ca/cm///vol3/no12/censorship.html> (August 18, 2006).

18. Personal interview with Bette Keller, August 27, 2006.

19. Leonard Pitts, "Parents Group Censors Ideas By Stealing Library Books," *The Bellingham Herald*, March 5, 2007, p. A8.

20. "Why Books Get Banned—or—'Free People Read Freely,'" BBC, h2g2, 1999, <http://www.bbc.co.uk/dna/h2g2/alabaster/A199109> (April 10, 2007).

21. "ALA Intellectual Freedom Committee Report to Council: 2000 Midwinter Meeting, San Antonio, TX," January 19, 2000, <http://www.ala.org/ala/oif/ifgroups/ifcommittee/ifcinaction/ifcreports/ifcreportmw00.pdf> (April 10, 2007).

22. Robert P. Doyle, *Banned Books* (Chicago: American Library Association, 2004), p. 544.

23. "*He who destroyes a good Booke, kills reason it selfe*: an exhibition of books which have survived Fire, the Sword and the Censors," University of Kansas Library, 1955, p. 8, <http://spencer.lib.ku.edu/exhibits/bannedbooks/unitedstates.html> (April 10, 2007).

24. "Off the Shelf: Who Should Decide What Books You Read?" *The Washington Post*, September 24, 2002, p. C14.

25. Madeleine L'Engle, "Dare to Be Creative!" a lecture presented at the Library of Congress, November 16, 1983 (Washington, D.C.: Library of Congress, 1984), p. 30.

26. "Notable First Amendment Court Cases," *American Library Association*, n.d., <http://www.ala.org/ala/oif/firstamendment/courtcases/courtcases.htm> (February 28, 2006).

27. Ibid.

28. Ibid.

29. "Keyishian et al v. Board of Regents of the University of the State of New York et al.," n.d., <http://www.bc.edu/bc_org/avp/cas/comm/free_speech/keyishian.html> (March 12, 2007).

Chapter 4.
Madeleine L'Engle: "Dare to Be Creative!"

1. Madeleine L'Engle, "Dare to Be Creative!" a lecture presented at the Library of Congress, November 16, 1983 (Washington, D.C.: Library of Congress, 1984), p. 13.

2. Cynthia Zarin, "The Storyteller: Fact, Fiction, and the Books of Madeleine L'Engle," *The New Yorker*, April 12, 2004, Vol. 80, No. 8, pp. 60–67.

3. L'Engle, "Dare to be Creative!" p. 17.

4. Ibid., p. 23.

5. Ibid., p. 20.

6. Ibid., p. 30.

7. Madeleine L'Engle, *Walking on Water: Reflections on Faith and Art* (New York: North Point Press, 1980), p. 52.

8. Madeleine L'Engle, *The Summer of the Great-Grandmother* (New York: Farrar, Strauss, and Giroux, 1974), p. 123.

9. Carole F. Chase, "Words of Wisdom from Madeleine L'Engle," *The Writer*, June 2002, Vol. 115, No. 6, pp. 26–28.

10. Heather Webb, "A Conversation with Madeleine L'Engle," *Mars Hill Review* 4, Winter/Spring 1996, pp. 51–65.

11. Carole F. Chase, *Madeleine L'Engle, Suncatcher* (San Diego: Lurimedia, 1995), p. 148.

12. Madeleine L'Engle, *The Rock That Is Higher: Story as Truth* (Wheaton, Ill.: Harold Shaw Publishers, 1993), p. 176.

13. Donald R. Hettinga, "A Great Cloud of Witnesses," *The Swiftly Tilting Worlds of Madeleine L'Engle*, Lucy Shaw, ed. (Wheaton, Ill.: Harold Shaw Publishers, 1998), p. 166.

14. L'Engle, *Walking on Water*, p. 106.

15. "President Bush Awards 2004 National Humanities Medals," *National Endowment for the Humanities*, n.d., <http://www.neh.gov/news/archive/20041117.html> (June 24, 2006).

Chapter 5.
The Storyteller: L'Engle's Characters and Themes

1. Cynthia Zarin, "The Storyteller: Fact, Fiction, and the Books of Madeleine L'Engle," *The New Yorker*, April 12, 2004, Vol. 80, No. 8, p. 60.

2. Ibid.

3. Anne Lamott, *Grace (Eventually): Thoughts on Faith* (New York: Penguin Books, 2007), p. 9.

4. Jeffrey P. Bezos, "A Wrinkle in Time," *Academy of Achievement: Recommended Books*, n.d., <http://www.achievement.org/autodoc/bibliography/WrinkleinT_1> (July 6, 2006).

5. Mike Pinter, "Bridging to Infinity," paper for Department of Mathematics and Computer Science, Belmont University, Nashville, Tennessee, n.d.,

<http://www2.hmc.edu.www_common/hmnj/pinter.pdf> (April 30, 2007).

6. Rachel B. Miller, "A Wrinkle in Goshen: L'Engle to address GC," *Goshen College Record*, September 12, 1996, <http://www.geocities.com/Athens/Acropolis/8838/goshrec.html?200621> (March 21, 2006).

7. *Women Writers of Children's Literature*, Harold Bloom, ed. (Philadelphia, Penn.: Chelsea House, 1998), p. 72.

8. *Madeleine L'Engle: Star*Gazer,* Videotape produced and directed by Martha Wheelock (Studio City, Calif.: Ishtar Films, 1990).

9. Madeleine L'Engle, *Walking on Water: Reflections on Faith and Art* (New York: North Point Press, 1980), p. 109.

10. Ibid., p. 114.

11. *Madeleine L'Engle: Star*Gazer.*

12. Madeleine L'Engle, *A Circle of Quiet* (New York: Farrar, Straus and Giroux, 1972), p. 93.

13. L'Engle, *Walking on Water*, p. 186.

14. Carole F. Chase, *Madeleine L'Engle, Suncatcher* (San Diego: Lurimedia, 1995), p. 44.

15. Ibid.

16. Ibid., p. 144.

17. L'Engle, *A Circle of Quiet*, p. 97.

18. L'Engle, *Walking on Water*, p. 34.

19. Ibid., p. 182.

20. *Madeleine L'Engle: Star*Gazer.*

21. L'Engle, *A Circle of Quiet*, p. 89.

Chapter 6.
A Wrinkle in Time

1. Madeleine L'Engle, *A Wrinkle in Time* (New York: Bantam Doubleday Dell Publishing Group, Inc., 1973), p. 3.

2. Ibid., p. 21.

3. Ibid., p. 36.

4. Ibid., p. 37.

5. Claris Van Kuiken, *Battle to Destroy Truth* (Manassas, Va.: REF Publishing, 1996), p. 54.

6. Ibid., p. 55.

7. "Camazotz," *Metareligion*, n.d., <http://www.meta-religion.com/Paranormale/Cryptozoology/Other/camazots.htm> (March 26, 2007).

8. Carole F. Chase, *Madeleine L'Engle, Suncatcher* (San Diego: Lurimedia, 1995), p. 38.

9. *Madeleine L'Engle: Star*Gazer*, Videotape produced and directed by Martha Wheelock (Studio City, Calif.: Ishtar Films, 1990).

10. Karen Pritzker, "Writer Hero: Madeleine L'Engle," *My Hero Project*, n.d., <http://myhero.com/myhero/hero.asp?hero=engle> (March 21, 2006).

11. Virginia L. Wolf, "Readers of Alice: My Children, Meg Murry, and Harriet M. Welsch," *Women Writers of Children's Literature*, Harold Bloom, ed. (Philadelphia, Penn.: Chelsea House, 1998), p. 76.

12. Madeleine L'Engle, *A Circle of Quiet* (New York: Farrar, Straus and Giroux, 1972), p. 24.

13. Ibid., p. 218.

Chapter 7.
Many Waters

1. Madeleine L'Engle, *Many Waters* (New York: Dell Yearling, 1986), p. 9.

2. Madeleine L'Engle, *And It Was Good: Reflections on Beginnings* (Wheaton, Ill.: Harold Shaw, 1983), p. 25.

3. Cathleen Rountree, *On Women Turning 70: Honoring the Voices of Wisdom* (San Francisco, Calif.: Jossey-Bass, 1999), p. 105.

4. Madeleine L'Engle, *A Circle of Quiet* (New York: Farrar, Straus and Giroux, 1972), p. 206.

5. L'Engle, *Many Waters*, p. 169.

6. Ibid., p. 296.

7. Ibid., p. 304.

8. Ibid., p. 299.

9. Ibid.

Chapter 8.
Challenges to L'Engle's Work

1. "Challenged and Banned Books," *American Library Association*, n.d.,<http://www.ala.org/ala/oif/bannedbooks week/challengedbanned/challengedbanned.htm> (March 29, 2007).

2. Ibid.

3. Ibid.

4. "Background," n.d., <http://www.ala.org/ala/oif/ban nedbooksweek/backgroundb/background.htm> (August 13, 2006).

5. Dan Cherubin, "Banned Books Week: Creating the Acceptable Taboo," *Counterpoise*, Gainesville, October 2003, Vol. 7, No. 4, p. 10.

6. "Focus on the Family Exposes the 'Banned' Books Lie," n.d., <http://www.family.org/welcome/press/a0022343. cfm> (August 11, 2006).

7. Madeleine L'Engle, *A Wrinkle in Time* (New York: Bantam Doubleday Dell Publishing Group, Inc., 1973), p. 89.

8. Herbert N. Foerstel, *Banned in the U.S.A.: A Reference Guide to Book Censorship in Schools and Public Libraries* (Westport, Conn.: Greenwood Press, 1994), p. 169.

9. *Attacks on the Freedom to Learn: 1989–1990 Report*, People for the American Way, Washington, D.C., 1990, p. 71.

10. *Attacks on the Freedom to Learn: 1990–1991 Report*, People for the American Way, Washington, D.C., 1991, p. 108.

11. Ibid., p. 20.

12. *Attacks on the Freedom to Learn: 1991–1992 Report*, People for the American Way, Washington, D.C., 1992, p. 40.

13. Ibid., p. 66.

14. Ibid., p. 86.

15. *Attacks on the Freedom to Learn: 1993–1994 Report*, People for the American Way, Washington, D.C., 1994, p. 51.

16. Foerstel, p. 260.

17. *Attacks on the Freedom to Learn: 1995–1996 Report*, People for the American Way, Washington, D.C., 1996, p. 211.

18. Ibid., p. 261.

19. Charles Suhor, "Recent SLATE Anti-Censorship Actions," *From the Front Line*, National Council of Teachers of English, October 1999, <http://www.ncte.org/library/files/about_ncte/issues/99_oct_front.pdf?source=gs> (March 1, 2007).

20. Letter from Nanette Perez, Project Coordinator, American Library Association, August 21, 2006.

21. *Banned Books Week '99*, American Library Association (Chicago: Jade Publishing, 1999), p. 60.

22. Letter from Nanette Perez.

23. Carole F. Chase, *Madeleine L'Engle, Suncatcher* (San Diego: Lurimedia, 1995), p. 14.

24. Madeleine L'Engle, *And It Was Good: Reflections on Beginnings* (Wheaton, Ill.: Harold Shaw, 1983), p. 49.

25. Betsy Hearne, "A Mind in Motion," School Library Journal, Vol. 44, No. 6, June 1998, pp. 28–33, <http://proquest.umi.com/pqdweb?did=30133305&Fmt=4

&clientld=22133&RQT=309&VName=PQD> (January 25, 2006).

26. Madeleine L'Engle, "Dare to Be Creative!" a lecture presented at the Library of Congress, November 16, 1983 (Washington, D.C.: Library of Congress, 1984), p. 15.

27. Madeleine L'Engle, *Penguins and Golden Calves: Icons and Idols* (Wheaton, Ill.: Harold Shaw Publishers, 1996), p. 82.

28. Ibid., p. 83.

Chapter 9.
The Legacy of Madeleine L'Engle

1. Cathleen Rountree, *On Women Turning 70: Honoring the Voices of Wisdom* (San Francisco, Calif.: Jossey-Bass Publishers, 1999), p. 98.

2. Thomas Howard, "Of Imagination, Story and Reality," *The Swiftly Tilting Worlds of Madeleine L'Engle*, Luci Shaw, ed. (Wheaton, Ill.: Harold Shaw Publishers, 1998), p. 105.

3. Brian Andreas quoted with permission from StoryPeople, Inc., P.O. Box 7, Decorah, Iowa, 52101, 2006, <www.storypeople.com> (April 30, 2007).

4. Donald R. Hettinga, "A Great Cloud of Witnesses," *The Swiftly Tilting Worlds of Madeleine L'Engle*, Lucy Shaw, ed. (Wheaton, Ill.: Harold Shaw Publishers, 1998), p. 167.

5. Madeleine L'Engle, *Walking on Water: Reflections on Faith and Art* (New York: North Point Press, 1980), p. 44.

6. Ibid., p. 122.

7. Hettinga, p. 175.

8. Madeleine L'Engle, *And It Was Good: Reflections on Beginnings* (Wheaton, Ill.: Harold Shaw, 1983), p. 145.

9. Walter Wangerin, "Madeleine, My Eli," *The Swiftly Tilting Worlds of Madeleine L'Engle*, Lucy Shaw, ed. (Wheaton, Ill.: Harold Shaw Publishers, 1998), p. 221.

10. Personal interview with Luci Shaw, August 25, 2006.

Published works of Madeleine L'Engle

1944	18 Washington Square South: A Comedy in One Act
1945	The Small Rain (aka Prelude)
1946	Ilsa
1949	And Both Were Young
1951	Camilla Dickinson (aka Camilla)
1957	A Winter's Love
1960	Meet the Austins
1962	A Wrinkle in Time
1963	The Moon by Night
1964	The Twenty-Four Days Before Christmas
1965	The Arm of the Starfish
1966	The Love Letters
1967	The Journey with Jonah
1968	The Young Unicorns
1969	Dance in the Desert
	Lines Scribbled on an Envelope and Other Poems
1971	The Other Side of the Sun
1972	A Circle of Quiet
1973	A Wind in the Door
1974	Everyday Prayers
	Prayers for Sunday
	The Summer of the Great-Grandmother
1976	Dragons in the Waters

1990   *The Glorious Impossible: Jesus Christ & His Family* (illustrated with Giotto frescoes)

1992   *Certain Women*

1993   *The Rock That Is Higher: Story as Truth*

1994   *Anytime Prayers*

   Troubling a Star

1996   *Penguins and Golden Calves: Icons and Idols*

   A Live Coal in the Sea

   Wintersong: Christmas Readings (with Luci Shaw)

   Glimpses of Grace: Daily Thoughts and Reflections (with Carole F. Chase)

1997   *Mothers and Daughters* (with daughter Maria Rooney)

   Friends for the Journey (with Luci Shaw)

   Bright Evening Star: Mystery of the Incarnation

1998   *Miracle on 10th Street & Other Christmas Writings*

1999   *Mothers and Sons* (with daughter Maria Rooney)

   A Prayerbook for Spiritual Friends (with Luci Shaw)

   A Full House: An Austin Family Christmas

2001	*The Other Dog* (illustrated by Christine Davenier)
	Madeleine L'Engle Herself: Reflections on a Writing Life (compiled by Carole Chase)
2005	*The Ordering of Love: New and Collected Poems of Madeleine L'Engle*
2006	*The Joys of Love*

Glossary

agnostic—A person who believes that there is no way to prove beyond a doubt that God exists.

allegory—A literary device in which one thing stands as a symbol for another.

autocratic—Having absolute power.

blasphemous—Irreverent; having a disrespectful attitude toward God.

censorship—The suppression or removal of material that is considered objectionable, sensitive, or harmful.

conservative—Favoring traditional views and values; opposed to sudden change.

controversy—A dispute or disagreement.

copyright—The legal protection of an author's work.

divisive—Creating disunity or dissension.

doctrine—A body of religious or political beliefs.

evangelical—A conservative Christian point of view that stresses personal conversion and the importance sharing one's faith.

heretical—Having an opinion or practice contrary to established beliefs.

liberal—Open to change, tolerant of different views.

155

metaphor—A figure of speech; a word or phrase that compares one thing to another.

mysticism—A belief in experiences beyond the known world.

nephil—The offspring of a fallen angel; plural is *nephilim.*

New Age—An alternative spiritual movement with a variety of beliefs (such as reincarnation) and practices (such as holistic healing and meditation).

occult—The supernatural, mystical, or magical.

propaganda—Material distributed to spread a point of view.

protagonist—The main character in a piece of fiction.

satanic—Relating to the devil.

seraph—A type of angel mentioned in the Bible; plural is *seraphim.*

taboo—Forbidden, off limits.

telepathic—Able to communicate with the mind, without using the senses.

tesseract—A complex geometric figure with greater than three dimensions—a hypercube used by L'Engle to represent the folding of space-time to enable transportation.

theology—The study of the nature of God and faith.

Books

Doyle, Robert P. *Banned Books*. Chicago: American Library Association, 2004.

Farish, Leah. *The First Amendment: Freedom of Speech, Religion and the Press*. Berkeley Heights, N.J.: Enslow Publishers, 1998.

Karolides, Nicholas J., Margaret Bald, and Dawn B. Sova. *100 Banned Books: Censorship Histories of World Literature*. New York: Checkmark Books/Facts On File, 1999.

Ravitch, Diane. *The Language Police: How Pressure Groups Restrict What Students Learn*. New York: Knopf, 2003.

Rosenberg, Aaron. *Madeleine L'Engle*. New York: Rosen, 2006.

Weiss, Jaqueline Schacter. *Profiles in Children's Literature: Discussions With Authors, Artists, and Editors*. Lanham, Md.: Scarecrow Press, 2001.

Internet Addresses

Madeleine L'Engle Web site
<http://www.madeleinelengle.com>

Madeleine L'Engle collection at Wheaton College
<http://www.wheaton.edu/learnres/ARCSC/collects/sc03/bio.htm>

Index

Index